THOMAS HARDY

DOUGLAS BROWN

THOMAS HARDY

LONGMANS

LONGMANS, GREEN AND CO LTD
48 Grosvenor Street, London W.1

Associated companies, branches and representatives
throughout the world

This edition © Douglas Brown 1961

First published 1954
Second edition by photolithography 1961
New impressions 1961, 1962, 1967

PRINTED IN GREAT BRITAIN
BY JOHN DICKENS & CO LTD
NORTHAMPTON

To

THE MEMORY OF MY FATHER

PREFACE

THE biographical part of this study is brief, for Hardy was eminent both as novelist and poet, and the range, the interest, and the elusive quality of his achievement ask the major proportion of attention. Mrs. F. E. Hardy's *Early Life* and *Later Years*, a biography compiled largely from material prepared and arranged by Hardy himself, is fortunately still available; so is the shorter but no less valuable life by Edmund Blunden published some twenty years ago. In the absence of important fresh material it would anyway have been an ungrateful task to attempt again what has been well done already: moreover, since this book was written Evelyn Hardy's full-length biography has also appeared. The discussion of the changing climate of thought and belief in Hardy's time, and of Hardy's own intellectual development, is brief too. Sufficient weight has been allowed to these things already, and one or two helpful detailed studies are listed in the bibliography. There remains the need to establish the importance of quite another background to Hardy's work, agricultural rather than intellectual, and it is to this that I have addressed myself.

I am grateful to several friends who suggested improvements to earlier drafts of this study and to those who gave practical help in its preparation. I have been allowed to make many quotations from Hardy's novels, stories and poems, and from Mrs. Hardy's biography, by the kind permission of Messrs. Macmillan and Co., Ltd., and the Trustees of the Hardy Estate. I have not given page references for my excerpts because the editions readers are likely to possess differ from one another.

But I have tried to make the contexts clear enough for reference to be easy. I have italicized words and phrases occasionally in these quotations in order to clarify the discussion without repetition. Except where the contrary is expressly stated, all the italics in this book are mine. For permission to quote a passage from *Phoenix*, the collection of D. H. Lawrence's posthumously published work which includes his *Study of Thomas Hardy*, I am grateful to Messrs. William Heinemann, Ltd. For permission to quote a passage from R. P. Blackmur's *Language as Gesture* I am grateful to the author and Messrs. Allen and Unwin, Ltd. The historical works to which I am chiefly indebted are R. C. K. Ensor's *England, 1870–1914*, G. M. Trevelyan's *English Social History*, and—pre-eminently—Rider Haggard's *Rural England*.

In preparing the book for this edition I have made a number of minor corrections at several points, and more substantial alterations to the sections on *The Woodlanders* and *Jude the Obscure*. The essay on Hardy's poetry has also been revised, and its final pages rewritten.

CONTENTS

PREFACE   *page* vii

PART I: THE MAN
A BIOGRAPHICAL SKETCH   1

PART II: NOVELS AND STORIES
THE AGRICULTURAL THEME   29
NOVELS OF CHARACTER AND ENVIRONMENT   45
THE UNIQUENESS OF HIS ART   101

PART III: POEMS
THE HARVEST OF THE NOVELS   145

SELECT BIBLIOGRAPHY   185
INDEX   195

A BIOGRAPHICAL SKETCH

THOMAS HARDY was born of old Dorset stock at Higher Bockhampton, a hamlet in the parish of Stinsford, near Dorchester, on 2 June 1840. His father was a master mason, sufficiently thriving, and life-holder of his own house and property at Bockhampton. The social status of a mason in a secluded part of Dorset was not high. At one time, the Hardys had stood far higher in village society. Thomas Hardy, married in later life to the daughter of an Archdeacon, and often resident in London, acquainted with eminent men and women, never lost either his sense of social inferiority or his loyalty to his father's kin. Once he had left the country to become a Londoner, he experienced the unrest and nostalgia of those who lack a social group to which they can truly belong. The sense of divided loyalties troubled him continually, and the novels reveal an acute consciousness of class—particularly the inferior novels whose material is close to autobiography.

His father was a buoyant, kindly man, passionately fond of music, a violinist and a singer much in demand at festivities. For many years before Thomas Hardy's birth the family had presided over the Church's music at Stinsford, where in the early forties a small orchestra still accompanied services. As a mason this devoted musician was unambitious. He loved Stinsford, and never left it, so denying himself the opportunity to rise in his trade. Mrs. Hardy was more ambitious. She came of a family very fond of reading, a sympathetic, stimulating woman, whose store of memories was even more remarkable than her husband's. In later years Thomas Hardy turned frequently to his parents for refreshment; they were fast-rooted in an older and more stable world.

As an old man he used to say how much he owed to the wisdom and guidance of his mother, and to the reading she suggested. But he inherited, too, his father's love of music. He was of an ecstatic temperament, and some of the folk-dance tunes stirred him to tears. He learnt to fiddle while still young, and took a share in the music-making at village festivities. He became acquainted with the rigours as well as the rewards of farming life. He never forgot the boy labourer who died of starvation and was found under a hedge, or the woman who was publicly hanged at Dorchester for a *crime passionel*, or the ravages of cholera in the wretched and unsanitary dwellings of villages near Dorchester. His nearer contacts, however, were with the educated group within the community—the vicar at Stinsford, his two sons, the schoolmistress, and the lady of the manor (for whom he long nursed a devoted ardour).

The village school where he began his education was a good one, and his mother encouraged his precocious reading tastes. Then he went on to the High School at Dorchester. He was, at this time, a solitary and thoughtful boy, who enjoyed taking the daily walk from Bockhampton to Dorchester alone. The walks, whether by daylight or in darkness, left with him a store of memories. During these years, his attachment to his native surroundings grew deep. Mr. Blunden has put the point eloquently: 'All that Hardy felt and reasoned about mankind was founded in a particular apprehension of "local hearts and heads". His absolutes were conjectured first and last from a profound submission to the diurnal visible microcosm of Wessex.'

Thomas Hardy's father was a friend of the Dorchester architect, John Hicks. At sixteen, the boy was frail for his years, and his future career was something of a problem for the family. Hicks solved the problem by taking him on as a pupil. He was a good master, sensible and kind, and a well educated man. He trained Hardy well, and yet left him leisure enough to pursue his other studies. Hardy continued to live at home, walking daily from Bockhampton to Dorchester as during his school-days. During the summer months, he would rise in the early hours to read, before setting out for the town. Next door to Hicks's office, William Barnes, the poet and philologist, kept a school. To him Hardy and his fellow apprentice took their intellectual problems and arguments, and Hardy conceived for him an affection and admiration he never lost. These were happy years. He combined, he would say later, in the twenty-four hours of a day, the professional life, the scholar's life, and the rustic life. When his fellow-student left the office for London Hardy found another friend, one who had the profoundest influence upon his mind and his spiritual development. Horace Moule was older than Hardy, a classical scholar of Queens' College, Cambridge, now starting life independently as a free-lance essayist and reviewer. He was a son of the vicar of Fordington, and the family was one of distinction. The vicarage society must have stimulated Hardy. The vicar himself had long since impressed Mrs. Hardy, and Thomas Hardy always remembered how bravely he had managed during the time of the cholera ravages. In 1854 this clergyman, whose grasp of agricultural economy and knowledge of

Dorset conditions were exceptional, had published a series of *Letters to His Royal Highness Prince Albert on the Dwellings and Condition of Eleven Hundred of the Working Classes and Poor of Fordington*. Hardy remained a lifelong friend of several of the family.

Horace Moule was the most gifted of all the brothers. He had a brilliant mind, and his teaching and his talk cast, so it was said, some indefinable glamour over books and learning. Before they became friends, Hardy had taught himself Greek, and read the *Iliad* and some Attic tragedy. Now, Moule talked frequently with him of Greek literature, and at the same time introduced him to contemporary issues of thought and faith. He guided some of Hardy's reading and study; and he sympathized with his aspiration to become an author. Hardy had written a good deal of verse already, but Moule dissuaded him from attempting to publish too quickly. Hardy began to grapple earnestly with the difficulty of reconciling religious belief with the modern outlook; Horace Moule remained a convinced Christian, an admirer of the liberal theologians. His influence with Hardy was for many years paramount. But it was an equivocal influence. During the years of their friendship personal tragedy overcast Moule's life, and he suffered periods of intense melancholy, a kind of suffering that cannot have been without its effect upon Hardy. At twenty-two, his training in Dorchester complete, he went to London, to advance both his architectural and his literary ambitions. He joined the staff of a flourishing young architect named Arthur Blomfield, a man of great kindness and insight, and a keen musician. He began regular work as a journeyman in the drawing office. In his spare time he read widely, attended lectures, and went to concerts and picture galleries. From time to time he met Horace Moule, who continued to direct

his reading, but advised him to give up Greek and concentrate upon his architectural training. The writings
of Huxley and Mill, and the discussions in periodicals
such as *The Saturday Review* to which Moule contributed,
made a deep impression upon him. London long continued to bewilder, even, at times, to frighten him.
Gradually his loneliness lifted, but not his social discomfort. He was not happy. In his profession he worked
steadily, but with less and less ambition. The manners
and life of the smarter set in London repelled him, and
his political convictions took a Radical turn. Authorship
was his aim, and he discussed the different openings with
Moule. He won the R.I.B.A. Prize for an essay on *The
Application of Coloured Bricks and Terra Cotta in Modern
Architecture*.

At Moule's suggestion he read Newman's *Apologia*—
'with a great desire to be convinced by him because
Moule likes him so much'. But Hardy was not convinced.
Modern enquiry, and more particularly the writings of
J. S. Mill, were undermining his religious faith. Then,
for a while, he abandoned all other forms of study in
order to devote himself to the reading of poetry. By
1865 he was convinced that to be a poet was his vocation;
and through all the chances of the next thirty years that
conviction remained. On 2 June of that year, he wrote
in his diary, 'My 25th birthday: not very cheerful. Feel
as if I had lived a long time and done very little. Walked
about by moonlight in the evening. Wondered what
woman, if any, I should be thinking about in 5 years'
time.' Not only was he depressed; hard study and the
conditions of life in London had weakened him. Blomfield suggested a country holiday, and, when a chance
request for an assistant came from Hicks at Dorchester,
Hardy undertook the work. In July 1867 he went back
to Bockhampton.

B

His health returned. He resumed his poetry, and continued to consider how authorship might be joined to the
career of an architect. As a result, he attempted something new. The contrast between the life he had
encountered in London and the familiar, traditional life
of the Dorset village became the basis of a first novel,
The Poor Man and the Lady. Hardy's perplexed sense of
class disparities, his Radical beliefs, and many of his own
experiences and memories thinly disguised or hardly
disguised at all, provided its substance. The novel gave a
harsh account of fashionable life in the city, enforced by
some incisive detail, evidence of watchful observation;
the country scenes were mellow and gentle, but no less
observant. By the beginning of 1868 he had completed
the fair copy, and he sent it to Macmillan. The letter
he received from Alexander Macmillan (it may be read
in his published *Letters*) was a model of scrupulous and
attentive criticism. Evidently he, and another reader,
had been much impressed by Hardy's talent; but the
book had faults, and he indicated both these, and the
dangers attendant upon a first appearance in print with so
candid and critical a novel. Hardy accepted an invitation
to visit Macmillan; but he did not enjoy the interview.
He took advantage of an introduction to Chapman and
Hall, and offered the book to them. Meanwhile he had
been executing small architectural commissions for both
Blomfield and Hicks, and in this independent way he
continued until Chapman and Hall undertook to publish
the novel if the author would put up twenty pounds.
Hardy accepted; but a long talk with George Meredith,
then a reader for Chapman and Hall, led to his with-
drawing the novel altogether. Meredith advised Hardy
to find his public with quite another style of narrative.
He recommended the study of Wilkie Collins. Later,
another publisher refused the novel, and Hardy put it to

one side. Some parts of it he rewrote and adapted for other purposes in after years, but in its original form *The Poor Man and the Lady* was never published, nor can it be adequately reconstructed. Hardy destroyed parts of the manuscript.

When Hicks died at Dorchester, another architect took over his practice. He invited Hardy to help him complete certain of Hicks's undertakings. Hardy agreed, and settled for a time in Weymouth. The quietness and the seaside air invigorated him, and he wrote freely during his leisure time. His second novel, *Desperate Remedies*, was of the kind suggested by Meredith. Hardy had nearly finished it when he received an urgent request to attend to the work of restoration at the Church of St. Juliot, near Boscastle.

There he met Emma Lavinia Gifford, whose sister had married the rector, and who had lived for some time at the rectory helping in parish affairs and the running of the house. She was a striking, athletic person, twenty-nine years old, very fond of riding, ambitious socially, and zealous in her work for the parish. Hardy stayed longer than was necessary, and explored in her company the countryside of Cornwall. She was so living, he used to say. Her vitality and her gaiety, and her deep interest in books, stirred him. After he left St. Juliot their friendship ripened. To Emma Gifford, Hardy was unlike anyone who came to those remote parts; he had the range of knowledge and the liveliness of mind she associated with the town. They corresponded; and she copied out for him parts of the new novel. He revisited St. Juliot professionally from time to time, and they met by arrangement in Bath and London.

Macmillan declined *Desperate Remedies* but another publisher, Tinsley, agreed to publish it if Hardy would put up seventy-five pounds. Bent upon the literary profession, Hardy agreed, and put all but fifty pounds of his worldly possessions into the publication. While in London, awaiting Tinsley's decision, he resumed close friendship with Horace Moule. Moule had spent a few years teaching at Marlborough; now, back in London, he was again reviewing and leader-writing. But private tragedy was plunging him into periods of gloom and despair. *Desperate Remedies* appeared anonymously. It is a striking novel, and the reviewer in the *Athenaeum* felt its power. The figure of Miss Aldclyffe and her passion for Cytherea can still make a deep impression: no common talent conceived the more violent scenes. There are masterly touches in the phrasing of the prose, especially the prose of some descriptive passages, such as the scene of the fire. *The Spectator's* review, however, was bitterly hostile to the novel. Hardy later admitted that the pain of the moment when he read that review remained unforgettable. Throughout the period of his novel-writing he remained acutely sensitive to criticism; only in the next century when, as a poet, he felt he was fulfilling his true vocation and need not care for the comments of others, did the sensitiveness abate. For the time being it was left to Horace Moule to restore his confidence. Gradually, and encouragingly, the volume sold. Hardy received all but fifteen pounds of the money he advanced.

Back at Bockhampton he composed *The Mellstock Quire*. More than any other of his books, this one celebrated the memories dear to him—the Stinsford memories. In later years he much regretted that he had not treated them in a more serious vein. For the present he was intent upon securing a public, and an income. The novel's material he chose partly in deference to the praise of Macmillan's reader for the rural parts of his unpublished first book. It was for fashion's sake, too, that he altered the title to the poetic *Under the Green-wood Tree*, thus (as with *Far from the Madding Crowd*) seeming to connect Wessex with the escape-world so dear to industrial England's iron time of doubts and fears. Emma Gifford again helped Hardy to prepare his copy. He sent it to Macmillan, with whom he still wished to publish. Again there was a close and sympathetic scrutiny, much admiration, and this time a guarded letter of acceptance. But Hardy misunderstood, and for the time being despaired of success in fiction. Instead, he turned back to architecture, secured several independent commissions, and worked very hard indeed. There followed a chance meeting in London with Tinsley, a blunt and forthright man whom Hardy liked, and a request for another novel. Hardy offered *Under the Greenwood Tree*, and Tinsley bought it for thirty pounds and published it forthwith. Uncertain of his future, Hardy still kept in close touch with Blomfield; by day he worked at architecture, and late into the night at Westbourne Park he wrote, and corrected proofs.

The new novel appeared in 1872. The reviewers received it well, and Tinsley worked hard to popularize it, for he was convinced it was both a good novel and a sound commercial proposition. But for many years sales were poor. Tinsley discussed with Hardy the finances of authorship, the demands of the fiction-reading public, and his own publishing ventures. He recommended serial writing for the periodicals as the one satisfactory financial basis for a novelist's career. Hardy closely investigated the proposals, found that this stunted version of a writer's calling offered prospects as secure as architecture could offer, closed with the publisher, and set to work to write a serial story for *Tinsley's Magazine*. He had composed a social satire, a mystery story, and an agricultural story; now he wrote a romantic story, one

which enshrined with much else his own Cornish romance. He ended his remaining architectural engagements. But architecture stayed with him, in another way,
for life. 'Those who have entered a church in Mr.
Hardy's company', wrote Mr. Blunden, 'may remember
the immediate sense of his mastery of all its various
material detail, as of its spiritual or emotional appeal,
which his look and manner and movement showed. The
training he had undergone meant an additional rightness
in his observation as a general habit, which was so valuable a resource in his novels and his other writings; the
singularities and visible strange histories of ancient buildings impressed on him, still young, the analogous un-
expectedness and incongruity of the fabric of human
affairs.'

Hardy strained his powers to keep up with the instalments of *A Pair of Blue Eyes*, and drew upon thinly disguised experiences of his own more and more readily.
This is, in fact, the first of those serialized novels of his
wherein it is not difficult to trace a sort of inner autobiography, and to detect the turning over and over of
certain private preoccupations. His second-rate work
provides the material for a more thorough study of his
emotional make-up than has so far been published,
although Mr. Guerard's book is full of stimulating perceptions. *A Pair of Blue Eyes* holds a strong narrative
interest, however, and contains several episodes both
fascinating and original. It is the most Victorian of his
books, and a few of his contemporaries favoured it
especially. Hardy himself—though he did not overrate
it—always kept a place in his affection for it; the glow of
his own romance was about it.

In 1873, after a fair success in its serial form, *A Pair
of Blue Eyes* appeared as a novel. Hardy had composed the
instalments at home; now he returned to London for a

while. He saw Horace Moule from time to time, and in the summer visited Cambridge, where Moule was resident for the time being. Hardy's diary records a 'never to be forgotten morning, very early, in King's College Chapel. H.M.M. saw me off for London. His last smile.' Hardy was at home again, in Bockhampton, when, in September, the news came that Horace Moule had committed suicide in his rooms at Queens' College. The depositions at the inquest, and particularly that of his brother, C. W. Moule, made it clear that some such tragic outcome to the long struggle with depression, anxiety and melancholy had been foreseen. For many years, but especially of late, he had tried to relieve his melancholy by taking spirits. Consequently the condition of depression and anxiety had become more acute; for he had felt that his professional career was in jeopardy, and had doubted his capacity any longer to carry out his work satisfactorily, or to order and control his life.

Hardy was profoundly affected. The memory of Horace Moule, and of the bitter suffering attendant upon so much ability and brilliance, never left him. It seems possible that the peculiarly grim details of the suicide are reflected in certain incidents in the novels. What can hardly be in doubt is the part Moule's figure had in the mind of the creator of Jude Fawley, and in the description of Jude's last months. Probably that figure had its part wherever, in Hardy's imaginative world, depression and despair accompany intellectual range and ardour.

Hardy's friendship with Leslie Stephen began not long after. Stephen too, during the years of their acquaintance, was to experience great personal suffering. It was a far less intimate friendship, but again it proved of great importance for the development of his mind and art. Stephen was the man, Mrs. F. E. Hardy wrote later, 'whose philosophy was to influence Hardy's own for

many years, more indeed than that of any of his contemporaries'. His was a penetrating and severe mind, and
from the first Hardy found him—although reticent, and
somewhat austere—congenial and stimulating. The
friendship began with a letter from Stephen, who had
been attracted by *Under the Greenwood Tree* late in 1872,
and discovered the author's identity from Horace Moule.
Stephen asked for a serial for his own periodical, *The
Cornhill*. Hardy sketched out for him *Far from the Madding Crowd*, and, stimulated by Stephen's admiration, he
set to work in happy leisure at home in Bockhampton.
In the autumn of 1873 he helped his father at cider-
making for the last time. Early next year, the first instalments of the story appeared in *The Cornhill*, although
Hardy had by no means completed it. As if to make
amends, the reviewer for *The Spectator* was the first to
welcome *Far from the Madding Crowd*. But towards the
end of the serial publication Hardy and Stephen differed
sharply about the concessions a novelist ought to make to
the tastes and prejudices of magazine-readers.

In August 1874, Hardy married Emma Gifford at St.
Peter's, Elgin Avenue. They spent their honeymoon in
France, and returned to live at Surbiton. Published as a
novel, *Far from the Madding Crowd* received many favourable reviews. Stephen asked for another serial; other
editors asked too. Hardy accepted two engagements, and
at the same time began to enjoy some of the pleasures of
London life with the wife he had released from the
fastnesses of Cornwall. Working against time, stringing
the episodes together, he composed *The Hand of Ethelberta*. He was in search of reputation and security, and
he was determined not to appear merely a provincial
novelist. But the new serial disappointed many admirers.
It had lively passages, but no consistent force and no
touches of genius. Stephen advised Hardy to neglect the

critics and to work his own vein; so indeed the novelist
was privately bent upon doing, as his notebooks make
very clear.

It seems likely that Hardy wanted a house in Dorset
while his wife, able at last to enjoy the pleasures of town
society, preferred to live in London. However, when a
cottage at Sturminster Newton, overlooking the Stour,
offered itself, Hardy secured it. Here, he and his wife
spent their happiest days together, as yet little troubled
by the disparities of temperament and darker shadows
which were later to sadden their union. But even here,
as he worked upon *The Return of the Native* meditatively
and at leisure, Hardy was oppressed. 'All is vanity, saith
the preacher', he wrote in his notebook. 'But if only all
were vanity who would mind? Alas, it is too often worse
than vanity. Agony, darkness, death also.' Memories of
Horace Moule may still have been present; or perhaps the
plight of Leslie Stephen, whose first wife had died suddenly, in 1875, leaving him temporarily numb with grief,
and later afflicted with melancholy. Stephen had refused
the offer of *The Return of the Native*; some parts of the
story Hardy designed promised to offend the public that
an editor had to please. As he finished the story, Hardy
began to feel afresh the precariousness of his position as a
writer. He felt isolated, and decided to move back to
London—a decision whose wisdom he afterwards questioned. There are two little entries of a more personal
sort in his notebook for this time. On 13 August 1877,
he wrote, 'We hear that Jane, our late servant, is to have
a baby. Yet never a sign of one is there for us.' Then in
March of the next year he wrote, 'End of the Sturminster
Newton Idyll.' Later on, he was to add, 'Our happiest
time.'

Hardy and his wife resumed an active social life in
London, and made many new friends. Edmund Gosse was

among them and he remained a close friend through the rest of Hardy's life-time. *The Return of the Native*, its end somewhat spoiled to suit the taste of its public, appeared later in 1878. When an invitation to write another serial came, Hardy decided to make preliminary use of some of the material he was busy collecting for the Napoleonic epic which seems to have been constantly in his thoughts. *The Trumpet-Major* made slow progress at first, while Hardy and his wife moved uncertainly from place to place, still looking for a home. When he had completed the instalments and prepared the book for publication, he took his wife to France again. Then a great physical weariness came over him, and he had premonitions of grave illness. *The Return of the Native* had not generally been well received; on the other hand, short stories solicited by editors, and costing far less in imaginative labour, added to his repute, and *The Trumpet-Major* was welcomed with enthusiasm. Leslie Stephen— rather perversely, Hardy felt, seeing that he had refused *The Return of the Native*—regretted that *The Cornhill* had not had the offer of the later novel. Back in London Hardy found himself far more secure financially, but more bewildered than before about the responsibilities of a novelist.

The next year found him an invalid, suffering from internal haemorrhage. While in bed, and despite much pain and discomfort, he dictated to his wife the greater part of his new serial. He determined to complete it somehow, for he had promised it to his American publisher, Harper, who had served him well, and was now bringing out a periodical in England. Moreover, Hardy could not help giving thought to the inadequate provision he had made for his wife, should he die now. *A Laodicean* had started vigorously; but the later parts, composed under such stress, reveal the poverty of invention one might expect. In some places the autobiographical transfer wears very thin.

After this illness Hardy determined to return finally to Dorset and to visit London only from time to time. His wife had nursed him patiently and loyally; whatever her private feelings about leaving London, she probably realized the necessity of country life for the better health of her husband. Hardy had found, too, Mrs. F. E. Hardy records, 'that residence in or near a city tended to force mechanical and ordinary productions from his pen, concerning ordinary social life and habits.'

Two on a Tower, his next serial, came out in 1882. It is the best of the lesser novels; it starts excellently, and some of the rural episodes are in Hardy's most successful light vein. But however sincerely and affectionately imagined, they do not compose the substance of the novel, and Hardy could not get the ironic manner designed for urbane social comedy into his prose for long at a time. This sophisticated novel succeeded well enough, however, and by 1883, with earlier books continuing to sell, Hardy's financial position was far better. In June of that year he bought an acre and a half of land near Dorchester, and set to work to design and build his own house. He lived in Dorchester during the time of the building of 'Max Gate', and began to compose his most ambitious novel so far: *The Mayor of Casterbridge*. He was under no contract for a serial, and he worked at leisure, and in familiar surroundings. Moreover, the *Westminster Review* had recently published a distinguished appreciation, *The Novels of Thomas Hardy*, by Havelock Ellis, and Hardy was much encouraged, as he had been by Leslie Stephen's admiration earlier. Health and vigour beyond any he had known for years sent his spirits soaring. He took possession of his own house at last, and there completed the novel. It first appeared as a serial, and later in book form, and it was very warmly received. Both here and in America, Hardy's fame grew fast.

He began work at once upon another serious novel, *The Woodlanders*. It was to become his own favourite. Again he worked at leisure, interrupted only by occasional holidays in London. To judge by *The Mayor of Casterbridge* and this novel, the possession of his own home, in the heart of Dorset, imparted something further of clarity and conviction to his vision. It is important to notice that the other two outstanding novels also belong to periods of settled residence in Dorsetshire, *Far from the Madding Crowd* to Hardy's last long stay at the family home at Bockhampton, and *The Return of the Native* to the years at Sturminster Newton. Fifteen months went to the composition of *The Woodlanders*, and when it was completed Hardy noted his reaction: 'Finished *The Woodlanders*—thought I should feel glad, but I do not particularly—though relieved.' In his imagination, Grace Melbury, the country girl who allies herself to the representative of the town world, and becomes uprooted, was doomed to an unhappy life with an inconstant husband. But—'I could not accentuate this strongly in the book.' Hardy's perplexed sense of the constraints put upon a novelist's sincerity to his vision took away something of the pride of craftsmanship and the joy of achievement. Still, it must have been a source of special satisfaction to him that *The Woodlanders* first appeared in Macmillan's Magazine.

The holidays in London had been taken more for his wife's enjoyment than his own. Both in London and at home, closer friends had become aware of some unhappiness in Hardy's personal relations with his wife, and of some periods of tension. Their mutual trust and loyalty remained; but in these later years he was not receiving the sympathetic insight that the first years had promised; on her side, she had found to her chagrin that she had not, after all, really married someone very different from the people she had known in Cornwall, but a countryman whose instinctive loyalties were to Dorset. She was much troubled, too, by his unbelief, for her own religious piety remained undisturbed.

In 1887 they travelled together in Italy; the next year they settled for a time in London. Hardy resumed his studies in philosophy, and read the contemporary German metaphysicians with particular interest. After another visit to Paris, he suffered a severe rheumatic attack, and in the autumn of 1888 the pair returned to Dorchester. With much distress of mind he began to explore afresh the Dorset countryside. It was by this time full of the signs of agricultural calamity and of abandonment. Then began the composition of *Tess*, at which he worked with great feeling. 'I have put in it the best of me', he said afterwards. When it was complete, both Macmillan and Murray refused to consider publishing it in their magazines. Hardy could not, even now, afford the financial loss of omitting serial publication. Dismayed and bitter, he mutilated his novel and sent it to a third editor, who accepted it. His mood alternated between cynical amusement and downright anger. But he resolved to abandon this trade altogether the moment he could afford it. Poetry was his vocation, and he had not wavered in that private conviction. All these years he had devoted what energies he could to writing poetry. He looked into the chances of publishing a volume of poems, *Songs of Twenty-five Years*. Then all such plans had to be laid aside in the new experience of notoriety that followed the publication of *Tess*. There was furious hostility, and there was vigorous partisanship. Earlier novels of his started to sell as never before. When the original *Tess* appeared, re-stored, in book form, it was more widely reviewed than

any other of his books had been. There were several
well-argued and sensible accounts of it; but there were
more indignant and unreasoned attacks. Ironically, this
tide of righteous anger turned out to be the means which
gained for the novelist sufficient financial reward to
enable him to turn to poetry for the rest of his life. The
novel continued to make a profound impression.
Wherever he went, said Gosse, he heard its praises. *Tess*
took Hardy to the forefront of living novelists. Lionel
Johnson's remarkable appraisal published that year, *The
Art of Thomas Hardy*, consolidated that position.

Hardy's father died at this time, and he began to feel
his own frailty. A silence had fallen between himself and
Stephen, 'a silence I shall always regret', he wrote after
Stephen's death. For Leslie Stephen's declining years
were years of great distress: the hereditary strain of
madness in his family was working itself out in a younger
generation. A period of visits and travels ended with the
winter of 1893; not long after, Emma became unwell.
Hardy was made vividly aware of how much his domestic
well-being depended upon her accustomed services.

When she had recovered, he explored north Dorsetshire and Oxford, before setting to work on *Jude*—
something, he wrote in his notebook, of the plot, 'something the world ought to be shown'. As the novel
developed, he knew that it would never do for the serial
public. Much of his time he spent working at the revi-
sion of all his earlier novels in readiness for a projected
Collected Edition. Then he began to mutilate *Jude* for its
serial appearance, feeling, no doubt, that the end of this
confusing, frustrating business of composing novels for the
English reading public in the last decades of the nineteenth century was near. He had premonitions of the
trouble that might follow the publication of the restored
Jude as a novel. When in fact the onslaught did begin, he

covered his pain with a veneer of cynical amusement. But he resolved absolutely—financial circumstances now aiding him—against writing any more novels. 'You can hardly have an idea', he wrote to a friend, 'how poor and feeble the book seems to me beside the idea that I had formed of it in prospect.' It was characteristic of him— of his need for encouragement, of his modesty—that he wrote gratefully to the one or two serious reviewers whose more thoughtful accounts of the book came his way. But Emma could offer little sympathy or understanding. She had apparently made her own private attempts to stop the publication of the book.

Trying to forget *Jude* and the notoriety, Hardy and his wife travelled about the country, and visited the Continent again. The notebooks suggest that Hardy was thinking more and more of his projected work on the Napoleonic theme; and in that prospect, and the prospect of devoting his remaining years to poetry, he recovered his composure, and he and Emma experienced a brief return of happiness. He gathered, sorted, and revised poetry he had written over many years, while *The Well-Beloved*, composed for serialization before *Jude*, and based upon still earlier sketches, made its appearance. It is an original novel, certainly, but slight, and little characteristic of Hardy's gifts, and it has never been widely read. In 1897, after another short stay in London, he took Emma to Switzerland. There, one evening, the memory of the Great Shreckhorn which Leslie Stephen had been the first to climb came back vividly upon his mind, and he composed a sonnet of tribute to his friend. Diffident, as often, he kept it by him, and Stephen never read it. Then he was taken ill, and had to come home for a rest. When he recovered, he took to cycling and toured the countryside frequently, often with his wife. Then, at the British Museum, he completed his studies in the historical sources, and began to gather together the results of many years' reflection, of the noting of memories and anecdotes, of reading in metaphysics, of speculation upon the human condition. He was ready for the composition of what he believed would prove his masterpiece, *The Dynasts*. That the completed epic drama is indeed a literary masterpiece may be disputed; what seems indisputable is that *The Dynasts* represents the harvest of Hardy's thought and meditation, in the same sense as Ezra Pound intended when he called Hardy's poems the harvest of the novels.

Thomas Hardy appears to have been a serious and earnest, rather than a profound, consistent, or original thinker. His loss of traditional faith, his agnosticism, and his later pessimism about human freedom and human destiny, harmonize naturally with the movements of thought and belief predominant in his time, and with the particular contributions of some of his most distinguished contemporaries, thinkers and scientists. Yet Hardy had always pursued an independent course. This architect's journeyman mastered Greek and studied Attic tragedy before he read Huxley or Mill. He had noted how Crabbe laid bare the sordid miseries of ordinary lives; he had underscored some of the most despairing passages in Sophocles. Under the tutelage of Horace Moule, and in the mind of his time as he encountered it in London, he found intellectual confirmation rather than a revelation of unforeseen truths. With so many others, he adhered to firm moral standards and kept his conscience unusually sensitive, but without acknowledging any transcendent Cause as the ground of moral values. His private extension of the general insight is hardly a philosopher's; it sounds a note of protest, that of a baffled moralist. 'Pain has been and pain is. No new sort of morals in Nature can remove pain from the past or make it pleasure to those who bore it. So either . . . Nature is blind, or an automaton, and you only throw responsibility a stage further back.' His moral feeling is outraged by the indifference of nature to human values. But a profound sense of human responsibility remains. The very range and force of Hardy's later pessimistic beliefs imply firm convictions, something like the solid earth beneath the countryman's feet.

It is not difficult to trace a sort of intellectual history of the author of *The Dynasts*. Simplifying—but without seriously misleading—we may say that his agnosticism owed most to Herbert Spencer's *First Principles*, which was the source, too, for the conception of the emergent consciousness, a conception important throughout the epic-drama. In Darwin's writings he studied the evolutionary processes, and found evidence of the cruelty and pain apparent in the struggle for existence, one of his deepest preoccupations. But Huxley and Mill had the profounder effect upon him. Both were men to whom he gave a personal as well as an intellectual allegiance. Certainly Huxley influenced him profoundly in his abandonment of religious faith, and his alternative conviction that 'there is no alleviation for the sufferings of mankind except veracity of thought and action, and the resolute facing of the world as it is'. J. S. Mill convinced him that to be loyal to all the consequences of rational enquiry was an absolute obligation; that there must be no evasion of the problems posed by the existence of suffering and pain. Mill's suggestion that mind and sentience might have been produced unconsciously, particularly attracted Hardy. These four great men impressed him very powerfully, and he met and talked with many of their followers. Above all, his friendship with the searching, thorough thinker, Leslie Stephen, confirmed him in enquiry and conviction.

c

This is to emphasize the indebtedness of Hardy in the intellectual part of his search, and of his analysis of experience. In metaphysics and philosophy, early and late, he remained a student. The bent for abstract thought, and for the discipline of metaphysics, is a part of that seriousness and sincerity that he brought to human life and experience. He was as devoted as Stephen to the honest pursuit of enquiry, and then gradually he came to doubt the value even of that. By the time he had studied Schleiermacher, Hauptmann and Haeckel, and entered into his private despair, the framework of his thought was apparently one of nihilistic determinism. That the Cause of the universe and of life is blind, unconscious; that human life is a jarring accident in the natural order, and that human values are meaningless: these were the themes uppermost in his mind when he began to compose *The Dynasts*. The implications, as well as the fact, of Nature's indifference to human values, perplexed him. Only the countryman's pragmatic respect for a faith, a way of life, an ethic, sanctioned by time and tradition, lightened his darkness. 'An almost religious sense of the universe as against us, and not for us': that is Hardy's pessimism as it shaped itself finally. But his practical philosophy, he asserted, 'is distinctly meliorist. What are my books but one plea against man's inhumanity to man, woman, and the lower animals? . . . Whatever may be the inherent good or evil of life, it is certain that man makes it much worse than it need be. When we have got rid of a thousand remediable ills, it will be time enough to determine whether the ill that is irremediable outweighs the good.'

When his first volume of poems, *Wessex Poems*, appeared, Hardy sent a copy to Leslie Stephen, who had suffered greatly again by the loss of his second wife and by the sudden death of a daughter in the prime of life. The reviewers were mildly respectful, and Hardy felt sufficiently encouraged; for he had expected it to be supposed that a frustrated novelist had turned to verse. He worked at *The Dynasts*, continuing thorough in research so as to ensure that the epic-drama should have at least a substantial documentary value. In the summer he spent long hours cycling about Dorset, sometimes forty or fifty miles in a day. A second volume of his poems appeared, and by now a number of periodicals were glad to publish his verse, earlier and recent. He felt an inward serenity now that he could fufil his true vocation. He wished to be known, he told an American professor, as a poet who had written some stories in prose.

In 1902 he was still preparing drafts of *The Dynasts*. By the next summer, Part I was complete and in the hands of Macmillan, now the publisher of all his work. The epic-drama astonished many, and several journals received it with deep respect. Elsewhere criticism was hasty, even brash. Hardy was especially angered when the metaphysical conceptions behind the drama came in for ridicule. 'The very fact of my having tried to spread over art the latest illumination of the time, has darkened counsel in respect of me', he said. Before Part II appeared, his mother, stalwart and vigorous even in old age, and continually his counsellor, had died. When, with Part III, publication of the entire epic-drama was complete, public respect and acclaim exceeded anything Hardy had experienced before. So fame, and the outward honours that accompany fame, encouraged his advancing years. Aberdeen University conferred upon him the degree of LL.D., and he became President of the Society of Dorset Men in London. In Dorchester there was a dramatic performance of some scenes from *The Dynasts*, and frequently dramatic versions of the more famous novels came to the

London stage for brief periods. At the age of seventy, he received from the King the Order of Merit. When he returned to Max Gate, he was given the Freedom of Dorchester.

His third volume of poems had appeared by now, and he was living a more leisured life. He began to visit all the English cathedrals, and these visits continued through several years. A second time he prepared his novels for a complete edition, this time the new *Wessex Edition*. It was now that he grouped them so significantly, and composed the illuminating General Preface. A friendlier and more unconcerned attitude to the novels came over him as he worked. Then, in July 1912, Emma gave her last garden party. Her general health weakened, although she was still up and about in November. Suddenly she was taken more seriously ill, and within a day or two she died.

Hardy remained at Max Gate, his loneliness increasing, and his grief deepening rather than diminishing as weeks passed. As so often in his experience, deep-buried memories came to life. 'The scales fell from my eyes', he said later to Gosse. In a mood of distress he questioned his own part in the unhappiness of some periods of his married life. Had he done all that he should? Was the failure in some measure his responsibility? During these months he composed many of the loveliest of his elegies, later to be gathered together as *Veteris Vestigia Flammae*. He had written some poems about his wife, he told A. C. Benson afterwards, 'but didn't know whether to publish them or not. They were very intimate, of course—but the verses came; it was quite natural. One looked back through the years and saw some pictures; a loss like that makes one's old brain vocal.' Theirs had been a solidly founded union, a fundamental loyalty continuing on both sides. But there had been tensions. Emma's formal religious piety, her social aspirations, her occasional literary pretensions, and her strange blend of vitality and physical reticence, had driven him in upon privacy and solitude. But the sense of the division dismayed him. Something of her pride and waywardness, and something of his bewilderment, went to the making of the heroines of the novels. Moreover a tragic presence haunted their later years, the presence revealed in the poem *The Interloper*. There was some strain of insanity in Emma's family; and there were periods when she suffered some form of mental disorder. Hardy's loyalty to his memory of the best and most lovable in her, and his later reticence, have drawn a veil over the extent of her instability; we should respect the reticence without overlooking the distress and bewilderment Hardy suffered.

But now all was forgotten in the pain of loss and the sense of responsibility. Hardy's mind returned to the distant past. 'In spite of the differences between us,' he wrote, 'which it would be affectation to deny, and certain painful delusions she suffered from at times, my life is intensely sad to me now, without her.' Not least, he missed her ready management of practical affairs. His household became disordered, and unwanted visitors besieged Max Gate. Immediately after his wife's death he had summoned the help of Florence Dugdale, a much younger woman, and for many years a valued friend of the family, who had often undertaken secretarial tasks for Hardy. She came to Max Gate at once, helped in numberless practical ways, saw the funeral arrangements through, and quietly left. From time to time during the next year she visited Max Gate and gave what help she could. Her tact and understanding, her practical services, and her readiness to forget herself entirely if she could be of use to him, endeared her to Hardy. In February 1914, he married her, and from that time serenity and comfort returned to Max Gate. Florence Dugdale's devotion,

and her care for him, transformed his later years. No
second marriage could have made him happier.

Cambridge had conferred the degree of Litt.D. upon
him in 1913, and later he became an Honorary Fellow of
Magdalene College. He continued to compose poetry
freely; but with the outbreak of war he suffered a profound shock. He felt, once the catastrophe had come,
that it would not quickly end. He attended a meeting of
literary men, called to consider what part they could play
in setting forth the Allied Cause: the occasion impressed
him deeply. Another volume of his poems appeared,
and Granville Barker directed an interpretation of *The
Dynasts* on the stage. But the war, Hardy said later,
destroyed any belief he had left in the gradual ennoble-
ment of man. He continued, even in old age, to study
philosophy, and now he turned to the *Principia Ethica* of
G. E. Moore, and to the work of Bergson.

During the last years of the war, visits of younger
authors provided Hardy with a new sort of companion-
ship. He had in the past enjoyed the friendship of many
writers; for in these relationships he was singularly
modest and direct and unpretentious. Now he won the
affection of younger writers by the same personal gifts,
and by his naturalness and sincerity. He impressed some
of them very deeply. Mr. Blunden quotes an account of a
visit by Llewellyn Powys. 'He came in at last, a little
old man (dressed in tweeds after the manner of a country
squire) with the same round skull and the same goblin
eyebrows and the same eyes keen and alert. What was
it that he reminded me of? A night hawk? A falcon
owl? For I tell you the eyes that looked out of that
century-old skull were of the kind that see in the dark.'

Shortly after his seventy-eighth birthday, a specially-
bound volume of poems, tributes from some forty or
fifty living poets, was presented to him by Siegfried

Sassoon, and the honour moved him profoundly. His *Moments of Vision* had been published, and a volume of *Collected Poems*. Oxford University conferred the degree of D.Litt. upon him, and the University Dramatic Society invited him to watch its performance of *The Dynasts* in the open air. Mr. Charles Morgan's narrative of the occasion—reproduced in the *Later Years*—nobody will care to miss, who wishes to feel the strange spell this 'sprightly, alert, bird-like' old poet put upon the young. In 1920, when he was made a Fellow of the R.I.B.A., he paid his last visit to London. His birthday the next year was remembered with honour again. Dramatic performances of his stories continued, and he attended those he could. A film of *The Mayor of Casterbridge* was made, partly in Dorchester itself. We may well feel that Hardy's fiction lends itself ill to dramatization, but its potentialities in the medium of cinema seem exciting. Under the direction, say, of a Renoir (the Renoir of *The Southerners*) with a deep feeling for place and for agriculture, some qualities of the novels might be freshly illuminated.

Cycling or motoring, Hardy still explored new places and revisited familiar ones throughout Dorset. He continued to compose poetry, published another volume—energetically prefaced—and completed for the Dorchester Players a play in verse, *The Queen of Cornwall*. After a visit to Oxford (where Queen's College had made him an Honorary Fellow) in 1923, he did not leave Max Gate again. His life was leisurely and comfortable, full of memories, and much gladdened by the society of younger writers. Year by year the Balliol Players came to his home to present a Greek Tragedy for him in the open air. Often he haunted the old, familiar places like Kingston Maurward, where as a child he had listened to ballad singing, and Stinsford Church. Another volume of poems went off to the publishers, and two more years passed, serenely and sociably. There were now many friends to visit him, and many admirers: Max Gate had become a place of pilgrimage. He spent his eighty-seventh birthday with the Granville Barkers, and after lunch they left him for a while, to sleep. But—'We peeped in at him through the garden window. He was not asleep, but sitting, walled in with books, staring into the fire with that deep look of his.'

Until the end of 1927 he continued to write regularly. Then one day, sitting down to work in his study, he found that his strength was gone. From that time he weakened steadily. His final volume of poems, *Winter Words*, he had already revised and prepared for the press. Early in the new year, he died. His ashes were buried in Westminster Abbey, in the presence of a great gathering. At Stinsford, at the same time, and in the presence of a rural congregation, after a memorial service, his heart was buried in the grave of his first wife. At Dorchester another memorial service took place and all business ceased for an hour.

The respect and honour shown him by younger men gave Hardy particular pleasure during his declining years. One hundred and six of them signed an address to him on his eighty-first birthday. A part of it read: 'In your novels and poems you have given us a tragic vision of life which is informed by your knowledge of character and relieved by the charity of your humour, and sweetened by your sympathy with human suffering and endurance. We have learned from you that the proud heart can subdue the hardest fate, even in submitting to it. . . . In all that you have written you have shown the spirit of man, nourished by tradition and sustained by pride, persisting through defeat.'

PART II

NOVELS AND STORIES

THE AGRICULTURAL THEME

THE distinction of Hardy's novels is elusive. A careful reader is likely to find much of their prose unserviceable, even shoddy. There are fine passages, and even finer phrases, but even so it would be a difficult undertaking to demonstrate the claims of these books by direct reference to the writer's command and resource in the creative use of language. What other reliable evidence is there? Like the poet, the novelist contrives and constructs with words; but his language makes a cumulative effect. It works gradually, diffusely, and the whole to which it ministers cannot always be considered at a sitting. Hence the difficulty of quoting relevantly and pointedly from novels, and with that the difficulty of being confident in a critical discussion that the mind is encountering an object, some facet of a work of art that is really there. The difficulty is general, and with Hardy it is extreme. Quotation can only serve a limited purpose of itself, and the discussion of any passage has to be referred back to, and checked against, its full context.

These considerations have dictated the form and approach of the notes about some of Hardy's novels that follow, and of the attempt to give some definition to his achievement which concludes this Part. The novels I take to represent his strength are *Far from the Madding*

Crowd, *The Return of the Native*, *The Woodlanders*, *The Mayor of Casterbridge* and *Tess of the D'Urbervilles*. To these five, *Under the Greenwood Tree* makes a fitting prelude, and *Jude the Obscure* (where Hardy ranges so much more ambitiously) an impressive epilogue. One other among the novels deserves particular respect, the modest but effective *The Trumpet-Major*. To that, and to several of the more remarkable short stories, reference comes during the last section.

The five great novels have a common pattern. Lionel Johnson first suggested it and illuminated it by commentary. Hardy presents his conception through the play of life in a tract of the countryside. His protagonists are strong-natured countrymen, disciplined by the necessities of agricultural life. He brings into relation with them men and women from outside the rural world, better educated, superior in status, yet inferior in human worth. The contact occasions a sense of invasion, of disturbance. The story unfolds slowly, and the theme of urban invasion declares itself more clearly as the country, its labour, its people and its past consolidate their presence. Then the story assumes some form of dramatic conflict, strong and unsubtle, and the invasion wreaks its havoc. Human relations and human persons are represented less for their own sakes than for the clearer focusing of the invasion and the havoc. A period of ominous waiting may follow; what the situation means becomes more evident: it is a clash between agricultural and urban modes of life. From that point the story moves to its conclusion.

This pattern records Hardy's dismay at the predicament of the agricultural community in the south of England during the last part of the nineteenth century and at the precarious hold of the agricultural way of life.

It records a profound activity of the memory, a deep-seated allegiance of the writer's personality, a degree of dependence upon an identified and reliable past. This activity of the memory, and this dismay, directed and continually informed Hardy's imaginative fictions. We shall be in a position to read them more alertly and sensitively if we know something of the historical situation to which they owe their nature, and to which they witness: the agricultural tragedy of 1870–1902.

'Free Trade has filled the towns and emptied our countryside; it has gorged the banks but left our rickyards bare.' Rider Haggard is trenchant and eloquent in the *Conclusions* to his *Rural England*, a documentation of the state of our agriculture at the end of the nineteenth century. For the section on Dorset, Hardy himself contributed information and recollections. His record, said Rider Haggard, was sure to command universal attention and respect, 'having been given by one who, as all the world knows, has made life-long observation of this and kindred matters connected with the land'. What Hardy has to say, as one would expect, is moderate and balanced and enforced by detail. He is well aware of improvements in the labourer's lot, and of certain other gains; but aware also of the agricultural calamity of the past decades, and sensitive to the human loss involved. There is nothing in Hardy's evidence which contradicts Rider Haggard's summary: 'It is impossible to take a favourable view of the present prospects of the land, or of any class connected with it, in Dorsetshire.'

This situation forms the substance of Hardy's important fiction, and an important part of the experience behind his poetry. The twenty-five years of rural collapse and dismay were the years of the composition of his novels. The periods of time they cover nearly span the century; but the details of each refer directly or by implication to the contemporary environment, and the story of each makes imaginative comment upon the contemporary catastrophe. It is usual to investigate the mind and art of Hardy by reference to the intellectual and scientific movements of his age, and these have indeed their importance for the purpose. But Hardy is not a philosophical novelist; he disclaimed the pretension. Here it will be suggested that his narrative art takes both its material and its vitality from the agricultural, rather than from the philosophical, context. Those who know them already will recognize, in the account that follows, the substance of the *Novels of Character and Environment*. Those who have not yet read them, or who may turn to them again after a long lapse of time, are asked to believe that to read them against the background now to be sketched will be rewarding. The special character of Hardy's art will reveal itself more readily.

In 1846 Disraeli prophesied the ruin of agriculture as an inevitable consequence of Free Trade in corn. Two decades of apparent agricultural prosperity passed. Our farming developed in peace and security while abroad the Crimean War, the Franco-Prussian War, and the American Civil War conspired to stimulate our exports and to divert foreign food from our shores. Farming technology improved, the seasons were favourable, prices remained stable and fairly high, and livestock breeding prospered. Farmers and landlords repaired and rebuilt the farmhouses and outbuildings, and added new cottages to the estates. Rents and profits rose appreciably, but the labourer's wages did not, and during the winter the family often depended upon the easily exploited labour of wife and children. In Dorset and the south the weekly wage was sometimes less than twelve shillings a week.

Meanwhile railroads brought the towns nearer to countrymen, and a primary education designed to provide for urban life spread widely. In response to the lure of flourishing industry, higher wages, and the diversions and attractions of the towns, the exodus of agricultural labourers began. Agriculture was still our most important industry; it employed well over a million men. But this was a scattered labouring community, inadequately organized. Belief in union came slowly, but when at last Joseph Arch, a Liberal and a Primitive Methodist, a skilled agricultural labourer himself, pioneered an Agricultural Union, the movement spread. The National Agricultural Labourers' Union set itself to 'raise wages, shorten hours, and make a man out of a land-tied slave'. Conditions improved a little towards 1870, but the drift away from the land went on; the Union itself tended to settle disputes by planning temporary movements of labour, or the emigration of families.

The era of prosperity ended abruptly. In 1871 Disraeli was Prime Minister, but he had succumbed to the spirit of the times, and was bent upon commercial expansion and imperial power. Soon, home produce could not compete with imported foodstuffs. Prices fell, and farmers and landlords were gripped by uncertainty. Groups of southern farmers opposed the union in 1873 and turned off union labour, and employed blacklegs. There was a long struggle. The National Union enlisted help from the unions in the towns. But the farmers could make no headway against the depression, and held out. Strike pay ended, and bitterness spread throughout the union. Hope of the corporate strength that might have preserved the labouring community dwindled. Only the evident presence of an indispensable group within the nation, only the menace of a widespread unemployment throughout our agriculture, could suffi-

ciently have transformed the outlook of the political
leadership. Neither party was prepared to advocate the
drastic measures of Protection which alone (whatever
other consequences followed) could have saved British
agriculture.

As it was, the union movement in the countryside
weakened further, through internal dissension; member-
ship declined sharply; and the exodus to the towns continued. In 1874 wages fell again. And then the storm
broke. There was a general trade depression accompanied
by heavy imports of cheap food. The Franco-Prussian
war had ended; in America thousands had left the towns
to settle new prairies and to reap the first fruits of new
soil; the trade expansion that followed the opening of the
Suez Canal had receded. From 1875 until 1879 the harvests were very bad; in 1877 there was a severe outbreak
of rinderpest, and in 1878 hundreds of thousands of sheep
were destroyed by liver rot. Wheat cheapened annually,
and during this decade the area of wheat under cultivation fell by nearly a million acres. Sheep-farming
suffered even more severely, and only to a very
limited extent did cattle-farming take its place. By 1880
there were only 900,000 agricultural workers left.
Thousands had joined the 'general labourer' group in the
towns, and thousands more had emigrated with their
families.

In 1883 the first period of catastrophe ended with an
epidemic of foot and mouth disease which destroyed
hundreds of thousands of cattle. The price of wheat continued to fall; by 1886 it reached 31s. 0d. a quarter, and
only a million acres were still under cultivation. The
rich soil which bore heavy crops but cost most to cultivate
was the first to be abandoned. During the eighties
another hundred thousand workers left the countryside.
The depression had seemed to lift a little after 1884, but

in 1886 (the year of the publication of *The Mayor of Casterbridge*, a novel much concerned with the drama of the Corn Law conflicts) agriculture was ruined a second time. Imports extended to include frozen meat, cheese, butter and wool in large quantities. Farmers had exhausted their financial reserves, and Parliament could do nothing. Food was the currency in which other nations paid for the exports of our thriving industries; and cheap food was by now vital for the prosperity of workers in the towns and for the very survival of workers in the countryside. So agriculture continued to decline. Farmers could not afford the higher wages required to retain skill on the land, and to compete with the lure of the towns. Farm buildings deteriorated and good soil was laid waste. Changes came over the farming class itself. Families with traditions of good husbandry, who by thrift had survived the first depression, succumbed to the second. Yeomen suffered more than tenants, and those who struggled on reared less livestock and used less fertilizer.

By 1888 only 4,000 members of the National Agricultural Union remained. Old and disillusioned, Arch gave up, and the other pioneers followed. A year or two later there were only 750,000 workers left on the land, and the revival of trade in the later nineties drew more and more away. The acreage under cultivation still diminished, and during the two years when Hardy, at work on *Tess of the D'Urbervilles*, roamed the Dorset countryside, dismayed by the evidence of appalling disaster, buildings crumbled, fences collapsed, roads decayed, and farmhouses were abandoned. In 1893 a Royal Commission was appointed to investigate and report upon the national agriculture. During the next years it made three reports, in which the diagnosis was excellent, and there was virtually no prognosis at all.

Wheat prices fell to 26s. 4d., and then lower. By 1895 Hardy was writing *Jude the Obscure*, a novel concerned particularly with the breakaway from the village, with what the town really offered, with 'rising in the world'. For by now the desertion of large tracts of the country-side was no temporary matter; the scars were permanent. But the towns bred their own miseries. The lure wore off, as Jude discovered. These lost labourers faced disease, privations, unemployment and insecurity worse than any in the countryside.

In 1902, Rider Haggard's conclusions, buttressed by a truly formidable documentation, were dramatic but unqualified. Agriculture was still declining as the capital sums invested in it wasted. The farmers were impover-ished and were losing heart. Those whose pride in and conscience towards the land were greatest had suffered most; the countryside had lost many of its most respected figures. Lower standards of husbandry were inevitable. Speculators were buying up populous cornlands for con-version into uninhabited sheep runs. Piratical tenants were going from farm to farm exhausting the soil by taking without giving. The days of high farming, the days of the yeomanry, were beyond recall.

This account may seem to have elaborated too much; to have listed too many details, too many statistics. But the details are in fact the details of Hardy's novels, too often neglected or overlooked. Not only *Tess* and *Jude*, but each of the great Wessex novels treats in imaginative form of the defeat of our peasantry and the collapse of our agriculture.

This is not the place for a full discussion of the causes of the collapse. Our vast prosperity depended upon Free Trade and no other policy claimed serious attention. The very structure of the national trade hampered agricultural recovery. Industrial prosperity grew with the expanding exports of manufactured goods, negotiable for raw materials and cheap food. The first replenished the thriving industry of the factories, the second encouraged the thriving workers in the towns and made life more tolerable for the unlucky. Bitter though it seems, industry had an interest in the depression of agriculture. And behind the low prices of imported foodstuffs extended a situation over which Britain had no control at all. In America particularly, prodigious railroad expansion over wide prairie lands, a new abundance of steam transport at the ports, the favourable climates, the rich virgin soil and the new labour-saving machinery, provided overwhelming odds against our agriculture. We had no agricultural leaders; those who cared, and those who farmed, were impotent: and the feeling of human impotence is not strange to the reader of Hardy's novels.

The causes concern us little, here. But the human consequences concern us, as readers of Hardy, much more. The details have emerged already from the narrative of the decline. Under two headings a little more ought to be said. The tragedy of the exodus of the agricultural workers from the villages and the countryside, and what that tragedy represents, forms one of Hardy's continual themes. Its implications may be said to dominate his last novel. For the world imagined by these men and women never existed. They had long been accustomed to the idea of leaving the land; hearsay and the newspapers had suggested their own picture of the life of the towns; railroads had brought that life within grasp. Wages were higher, and they knew nothing of the cost of living. Hours were shorter, company more various, freedom and entertainment more abundant. The cottage accommodation of the countryside was bad, and they were not to know that in the slums and tenements

of overcrowded towns it was worse. The restless spirit
of the age, the insecurity of tenure, and the spread of
primary education, discontented those not already dismayed by evidences of decline. The rural education
which became compulsory during the last quarter of the
century was the off-shoot of a town system, and it
turned people to the towns as to the natural life. So
during the last years of the century it seemed that the
only chance for a young or enterprising person in the
countryside was to leave it. Then, uprooted, he found
in the towns casual labour or none, disillusion, and perhaps an old age of penury.

Secondly, behind the exodus, the desertion of the
countryside and the decline of husbandry, we should perceive a more fundamental issue. What will be the result,
asks Rider Haggard, where will it end? 'I will content
myself with a modest statement: it can mean nothing
less than the progressive deterioration of the race.' The
modesty is certainly disarming; but there is a substantial
weight of social analysis behind it. The national temperament, he believed, was undergoing subtle but profound
modifications; men's physique was deteriorating, the
quality of their intelligence was changing; they were no
longer apt to consider or appreciate natural things. 'If
high civilization necessitates a flight from the villages
then it is of a truth the broad road which leads to the
destruction of advanced peoples. England's greatest safe-
guard lies in the re-creation of a yeoman class rooted in
the soil and supported by the soil.' This account has
turned so frequently to Rider Haggard because he dealt
with the evidence at first hand, because he was so close to
the tragedy he documented and analysed, and because he
was near enough to Hardy himself to invite his collabora-
tion in the survey. For Rider Haggard, at least, the consequences of the agricultural tragedy are far-reaching. We

may well set by his account the testimony of a contemporary social historian. For Dr. Trevelyan, in *English Social History*, the collapse of agriculture was a major catastrophe. Contemporary thinkers and politicians believed, he says, 'that if one industry, agriculture for example, went under in free competition, other industries would gain proportionately and would take its place—and so all would be well. But all was not well. For political economy does not cover the whole field of human welfare. The men of theory failed to perceive that agriculture is not one industry among many, but is a way of life, unique and irreplaceable in its human and spiritual values.' A more important consequence than the change of economic circumstance, he adds, 'has been the general divorce of Englishmen from life in contact with nature, which in all previous ages had helped to form the mind and imagination of the island race.'

Hardy's sense of his subject and his responsibilities comes out clearly, if briefly, in the prefatory notes to the important novels. The same phrases recur: *have instituted enquiries to correct . . . have striven against temptations to exaggerate . . . have sought to preserve a true record of a vanishing way of life*. It comes out, too, in the little-known but important article he composed for *Longman's Magazine*, headed 'The Dorsetshire Labourer'—an article to which Rider Haggard pays tribute and from which he quotes. It was written in 1883, when the depression was acute. There are faults of tone and suggestions of condescension, in some places in the novels which might lead us to question whether Hardy the novelist does indeed treat the labourers 'as men with serious minds, problems, and attitudes, who live on wages', as Mr. V. S. Pritchett has rightly suggested he does. But in this article, though the novelist's gifts are in evidence, he does not fumble at all; his subject is presented with clarity and precision. Some passages and images linger in the memory, like the picture of the unattached labourer at the Hiring Fair, and the disturbing presence of the old shepherd, a symbol of the uncertainties shadowing old age under the new dispensation.

First, Hardy is angered by the stereotyped notion of 'Hodge' and by condescension towards agricultural workers. He contrasts the little revealed to cursory observation of country life, with the wealth revealed to patient, intimate attention. An unforeseen inner variety emerges, a style of living distinct from that of the towns. He goes on to deal with some human implications of the agricultural collapse and to examine the living conditions of attached and unattached labourers. His detailed sketch of Lady Day changes forms a persuasive image of a dissolving society. He is unsentimental about migrations, for he perceives certain gains: the new alertness, the education in the affairs of the world, the independence. In times gone by no answer was returned to the domineering landlord (none is returned at Flintcomb Ash, in *Tess*). Now, at least among travelled men, answer there would be. On the other hand, Hardy has his private feeling about the final result of 'education' and of 'insight into the conditions of existence'. A possible end was intellectual misery; perhaps also poverty, and the loneliness of exile from one's native community. So his level analysis of migration of labour has its sharper edge. Personal and clan characteristics get lost, he adds; and the humorous simplicity of the men and the unsophisticated modesty of the women. Hardy values the rustic character; but he does not value it as some of his critics (even among the most recent) have supposed, because it pleases his aesthetic curiosity. It is too much, he remarks tartly, to expect these men to remain stagnant and old-fashioned for the sake of a few romantic spectators. But with the loss of individuality goes a 'less intimate and kindly relation to the land they till,' and there is lost also the sense of community and of local tradition that goes with it.

The achievements of responsible squirearchy are in jeopardy, too. The sense of a mere sojourning, the profound uncertainties of land and cottage tenure, have moral consequences; they result in a more cynical view of the duties of life. The rural norm, Hardy implies, is vital to the moral stability of England. If we are to read with understanding those episodes in the novels which turn upon Lady Day migrations, the Hiring Fair, removal from house or cottage, loss of tenure, and so on (consider especially *The Woodlanders* and *Tess*), we have to grasp the implications of this insecurity.

Hardy ends his article with a sympathetic note about Arch, a summary of the real-wage situation for the agricultural worker in 1880, a note about the widespread dislike of the threshing machine, and a brief discussion of southern rustic humour. Finally, he returns to his main theme, the alarming depopulation of the countryside. So many skilled men have gone, and so many fine members of non-labouring groups long associated with their localities. 'The tendency of rural populations towards large towns,' he concludes, 'is really the tendency of water to flow uphill when forced by machinery.' The phrase, with others from this article, appeared verbatim in one of the later novels. The unattached elderly men and women, and the unwanted, are his last concern. 'The poignant regret of those obliged to forsake the old nest can be realized only by people who have witnessed it.'

Hardy was not, like Richard Jefferies, an inspired journalist of agricultural life as well as a considerable

novelist. And our valuation of the novels must, of course,
rest upon qualities perceptible in the novels themselves
and not elsewhere. But we shall be more perceptive readers if we reflect upon this agricultural tragedy,
the substance of his narrative art; and if we give some
attention not only to the prefatory notes, but also to this
one direct report upon the tragedy that Hardy made. It
reveals a confident intimacy with Dorsetshire agricultural
life, and a profound knowledge of what was dissolving,
and how, and why, and a grave feeling for the consequences.

Certainly Hardy's narrative impulse is partly nostalgic.
His best verse and some of his best prose have this in
common, that we can detect a disturbed and uneasy
memory working like a catalyst upon the substance of the
past. The recurrent image in the fiction of the invader
who menaces a stable, sheltered, but impotent community, and portends disaster, indicates the disturbance.
The country natures Hardy drew so memorably—Oak's,
Henchard's, Marty South's—impinge upon the reader's
consciousness from time to time with a certain urgency:
they answered to a deep need in their creator for reassu-
rance, for solidarity with a more secure, more limited,
more fortifying past. But whatever we allow to the
alchemy of memory, there remains as part of our experience of Hardy's finest characters a sense of their resilience; he has contrived them out of a strong, clear
feeling for the resource, the reliability, and the simplicity
of personalities nurtured by the traditional agricultural
society. There is a blend of nostalgia and imaginative vision.
And to whatever aspect of Hardy's novels we turn, in
some measure that blend confronts us. It is there most
obviously in his zest for the folklore that knits the community with its ancestry and its environment. Hardy

was most deeply stirred by the life he knew or heard of as a child; but in no part of the material of his art is there more particularity, more accuracy. His presentations of scene are most effective when revealing the country tract, aloof in space and time, 'outside the gates of the world'; but in those very scenes the eye and the ear are most perceptive and candid in their report. His preoccupation with the characteristic detail of place and trade, setting and activity, reveals a sort of dependence, a restricted devotion to a closed-in area of experience; but it reveals equally an unerring and intimate knowledge, and a flair for what will most readily convey the reality of a certain kind of livelihood. That flair contributes to his stylization of rural speech as well, and makes the speech more than an ideal and imaginary contrivance—though it is also that. The sentiment is not false, and the habitual watchfulness for detail is the countryman's own.

Because he knows the manners and techniques of the labouring vocations, and because he remains alert to the gradations of social status in the village and the countryside, Hardy gives body to his respect for the country community. The impact of the characters, too, comes partly through their author's grasp of their living conditions. Henchard's vitality expresses an appreciation not only of what he represents personally, but of his milieu as well. That is why the conflict with Farfrae is so compelling, 'northern insight matched against southron doggedness; the dirk against the cudgel.'

> His accounts were like bramblewood when Farfrae came. He used to reckon his sacks by chalk strokes all in a row like garden palings, measure his ricks by stretching with his arms, weigh his trusses by a lift, judge his hay by a chaw, and settle his prices with a curse. But now this accomplished young man does it all by ciphering and mensuration. . . .

Such perceptions about living conditions give force to touches of more apparent art, like the blending of the labourers' clothes with their environment or their toil.

Through Oak, Winterborne, Henchard, Tess, Hardy seeks to establish his intuition of the potential value of agricultural life, and to celebrate the naturalness of men and women engaged in the skills and necessities of agriculture. Henry James thought *Far from the Madding Crowd* had for its most genuine quality 'a certain aroma of the meadows and lanes, and a natural relish for harvestings and sheep-shearings.' So it has. But the relish is the eloquence of Hardy's feeling for the value of what he finds. Inventions like the experiences of Oak before the storm breaks, or the field labourers probing their way over Egdon in the darkness, inventions that connect men so intimately with their native environment, are at once urgent, elegiac, and yet full of substantial and accurate perceptions. They have a resonance which is Hardy's own contribution to our fiction, and which the next section of this study will try to explore.

NOVELS OF CHARACTER AND ENVIRONMENT

UNDER THE GREENWOOD TREE (1870–2)

THIS early novel, originally called the *Mellstock Quire*, reads like a first draft for the fiction of Hardy's maturity. Already productive agricultural life provides the essential material. The unanswerable condemnation of Thomas Leaf is the fear that he will 'never be able to tell how many cuts it do take to sharpen a spar.' The opening chapters are impregnated with affection for country life, and marked by touches of genuine discernment. *Under the Greenwood Tree*, in fact, is a novel to be taken seriously, even as it stands. Years after, Hardy wished his treatment had been as serious as the theme demanded. The book we have is admittedly faulty; it is marred by a facetious air that appears to be the off-shoot of the author's selfconsciousness. But its substance is important. Music counted for so much in the life of these communities that the choir's defeat represents a significant defeat. The choice Fancy Day has to make is similarly important. Perhaps the quiet, rather tentative quality of the story-telling, and the unassuming lightness about some (not all) of the humour, have done as much as the ponderous or disconcerting passages to make it easy to overlook the novelist's deep feeling for that defeat and for Fancy's predicament. That feeling gives the novel its distinction.

The old, stable order is passing from agricultural life: this is the impression made so vivid by the fate of the choir. The daily labour and the crafts and the music-making of these men and women are bound up with their traditional beliefs and customs. When the urban invader, Maybold, dismisses the choir, they are helpless and inarticulate before him. For a moment or two the scene stirs the depths. Hardy has contrived a felicitous image for his feeling, and he develops it reticently. The old order passes: and against the background of that passing we follow the attractive tale of Fancy and her three lovers. In various subtle ways—by her social status, her organ-playing, and so on—Hardy has embroiled her in the conflict. Continually in the course of the narrative, she reminds us of it. Tempted to turn from the agricultural society and 'to rise in the world' she conquers the temptation, succumbs, then conquers again. Hardy nowhere elaborates what is at stake while the girl delays, poised between Maybold and Dick. But you may sense in his narrative of her predicament the same deep, subdued feeling with which he regards the defeat of the choir.

But then, with what gay felicity he indicates the meaning of Fancy's final choice of Dick, the countryman!

> The same instant a small twig and flower from the creeper outside the door flew in at the open window, and a masculine voice said, 'Ready, Fancy dearest?'

Delicately and coolly the irony plays about the precariousness of the girl's decision.

> . . . The tranter, conspicuous by his enormous gloves, which . . . sat rather awkwardly upon his brown hands; this hallmark of respectability having been set upon himself today (by Fancy's special request) for the first time in his life. . . .

And at the end of the story, the narrative folds gently into an incident rich with metaphorical suggestion: the moment of hesitation, during the wedding festivities, between the old and the new fashion of bridal walk. The old is chosen, and Fancy and Dick move side by side

through the flowers. A similar suggestion hovers about
the tree which presides over the opening and closing
scenes. Old William's shadow comes to rest upon its
trunk at the beginning. At the end,

> Music and dancing and the singing of songs went forward
> with great spirit throughout the evening. . . . Whilst the
> dancing progressed the older persons sat in a group under
> the trunk of the tree. . .

That tree, a few paragraphs earlier, stood for continuity,
for the generations of the animals and birds. The sym-
bolisms of this tale, like the unfolding seasons that
colour its structure, are simple and direct; but the
feelings and insights they contain are delicate and genuine.

No doubt in places the faulty manner baffles the serious
intention. But we should attend first to the successes of
the novel, for the points of failure and the lapses of tone
are not thoroughly inherent. Take the interview between
the vicar and the choir. The preliminary over-emphasis,
the effects of brittle caricature, and particularly the
use of Leaf, do spoil the texture. But what engaging
subtlety follows, when the old ways of conducting affairs,
and the traditional social manners, collapse in embarrassment before the urban parson! The mutual unhappiness
is most delicately recorded.

The insecurity of Fancy's poise is the imaginative
centre of *Under the Greenwood Tree*. This insecurity
remains to the end, illuminating and reflecting the wider
rural insecurity. The music and dancing at the wedding
of Fancy with the countryman remind us over again of
the defeat of the choir; and that defeat dramatizes a more
general impotence. But Fancy's choice does counter
that defeat. And the weave of the tales, and of story
with seasons, suggests (with an art a shade too apparent)
that although the old, stable order is passing, the sources
for restoration may still be tapped. The loss, the dis-

may, is not yet tragic, and the deliberate framing of
the tale to suggest hope balances the insistence upon
dying traditions. Meanwhile, alike in the defeat of the
choir and in the momentary fall of Fancy, Maybold,
the lonely urban invader, is the responsible yet strangely
passive agent.

FAR FROM THE MADDING CROWD (1873–4)

Far from the Madding Crowd is a true sequel to *Under the
Greenwood Tree*, but it is a much more considerable performance. Compared with Bathsheba, Fancy seems the
slightest of studies. A second time Hardy images the
predicament of the sensitive, intelligent rural person inse-
curely poised between the country life to which she
belongs and the city milieu that her imagination tantalizes her with. Hardy is not generally profound or explora-
tory in his analysis of human character and motive. His
narrative art calls rather for a strong, simple delineation,
one that convinces the reader by confident definition.
The imaginative sympathy, and the certain touch, of the
strokes that compose the portrait of Bathsheba, have
often been appreciated. Yet Hardy's skill is (in the best
sense) conventional; it uses and blends both the conventions of the balladist and those of the Victorian novel.
Occasionally the aural and visual effects are less conventional. Bathsheba's various styles of speech are
finely discriminated: essaying fine manners with Bold-
wood, or patronage with Oak, or masculine forthright
authority with the labourers, or feminine authority with
Liddy. And from time to time we catch the voice of the
mere country girl. With a keen eye, too, Hardy
catches the indicative movement or gesture. These things
vindicate his grasp of village psychology, and illuminate
the limits within which his narrative art functions most

happily. Take, for instance, the ballad-like scene of the despatch of the Valentine. Bathsheba dominates the novel, not as a human personality created and explored with the searching art of the classical novelist, but as someone present to a balladist's imagination, confidently taken for granted as what she seems to be, recognized by the gesture of the hand, the inflexion of the voice; even the gradual transformation of her nature under the impress of suffering Hardy reveals in broad dramatic strokes. If ever she seems ineffective it is because the novelist has paused to explain her in an alien style.

It is again a ballad-tale he has to tell: a choice between the country squire, the loyal henchman, and the gay, enticing soldier, the invader from without. The agricultural context controls the force of the tale. The choral interludes of the fields and the malthouse take their quality from the country rituals and activities they celebrate—the birth of calves and lambs, the seasons of the fair, of the harvest, the sheepwashing, the grinding, the incising, the shearing, the hiving. These activities culminate in the intenser activity of emergency: the binding and covering and thatching of the ricks in the hour of darkness menaced by immense storm. This episode assumes a far richer symbolic power than any in the earlier novel.

The ruminations of the labourers take authenticity from their doings, not from the literary style in which they are cast. Hardy's sense of the facts of village life is far more important then his concealed memories of Shakespeare's rustics.

> 'And how was the old place at Norcombe when ye went for your dog? I should like to see the old familiar spot; but faith, I shouldn't know a soul there now.'
> 'I suppose you wouldn't. 'Tis altered very much.'

'Is it true that Dicky Hill's wooden cider-house is pulled down?'

'Oh yes—years ago, and Dicky's cottage just above it.'

'Well, to be sure!'

'Yes; and Tompkins's old apple-tree is rooted that used to bear two hogsheads of cider, and no help from other trees.'

'Rooted?—you don't say it! Ah! stirring times we live in—stirring times.'

'And you can mind the old well that used to be in the middle of the place? That's turned into a solid iron pump with a large stone trough, and all complete.'

'Dear, dear—how the face of nations alter—and what we live to see nowadays. Yes, and 'tis the same here. . . .'

The stylization is flawed, the whole manner over-insistent. Hardy sheds some weaknesses in the later novels. But even here the writing contains a serious attitude; we have to recognize the implications of destroyed cottages and migrating village communities. We should let these choric interludes simply direct our interests. A rustic eloquence we may distrust yet points towards things as trustworthy as the sheep-shearing scene. Those buoyant pages carry a concluding comment from the novelist:

In these Wessex nooks the busy outsider's ancient times are only old; his old times are still new; his present is futurity.

His present is futurity. There's the sting. What is Now for the busy outsider in 1874 is the countryman's To Come. 'The greatest single event of the seventies, fraught with immeasurable consequences for the future, was the collapse of agriculture.' (Trevelyan.) In the meantime, (and do we not sense the ache?) 'the barn was natural to the shearers, and the shearers were in harmony with the barn.'

Such is the pattern of this novel. Inventions like the

sheep-shearing scene give body to the choric ruminations of the labourers. These in turn point out the wider implications of the agricultural skills and traditions in the moment of the precipitate decline of the agricultural society. And the whole context illuminates the meaning of the tale of Bathsheba's bitter choice. When, for instance, Cain Ball speaks of his experiences in the city of Bath, the pivotal tragedy of the tale (when Bathsheba chooses the invading lover, and with him flies from the country to that city) and the gathering weight of the details and crafts and traditions of Weatherbury life, combine in a single impression. 'The boy's maning', they conclude,

> 'is that the sky and the earth in the kingdom of Bath is not altogether different from ours here. 'Tis for our good to gain knowledge of strange cities. . . .'

A sufficient embodiment of 'ours here' has entered into the texture of the novel. The sense of distance is real. Troy has dazzled and beguiled with the flash of his sabre ; Oak has served and saved with the shepherd-surgeon's needle.

The feeling of division has its more compelling imagery in the festivity of the evening before the storm, and during the storm. In such a sequence we may detect the special grace of this book. First, there is Oak, 'motionless in the stackyard, looking'. Hardy's description of the signs of the night sky reveals a striking expenditure of effort. The body of apprehension seems to be just beyond the finger-tips of language. 'Thunder was imminent', the passage ends, ' . . . likely to be followed by heavy rains. Oak gazed at eight naked and unprotected ricks, massive and heavy with the rich produce of one half the farm for that year. He went on to the farm.' The traditional revel takes place against this background. The situation con-

nects obviously enough with the larger, deliberate irony
of the story; but it has a subdued, tough irony of its own.
Harvest Home is celebrated while a storm gathers over
unprotected ricks. Moreover this festival reminds the
reader of the sheep-shearing supper, the earlier feast of
spontaneous mirth presided over by the farmer, the
shepherd, and a neighbouring farmer. This feast, which
ought also to be mirthful, has become an occasion for
artificial goodwill. The bright, beguiling visitor from
an alien kingdom prompted it and presides over it, to
celebrate, not harvest, but his marriage with the
country girl and his usurpation of country rule. The
first dance of this Harvest Home is called 'The Soldier's
Joy', and when Oak enters with his warning message
he finds Troy drinking brandy while the labourers take
cider and ale.

> 'Mr. Troy says it will not rain,' returned the messenger,
> 'and he cannot stop to talk to you about such fidgets.'

Side by side with the arrogant soldier, Oak looked
'like a candle beside gas', Hardy comments curtly. The
narrative style achieves here the candour and directness
that came when the novelist's deepest feelings found
release in imagery perfectly adjusted to them, and he
could write with unusual absorption. Brandy circulates
freely; long-sanctioned customs are disregarded. The
women and children leave. So does Bathsheba. So do
the musicians, 'not looking upon themselves as company.'
The phrases tingle with delicate implications.

The prose of fiction has a serial effect. One group
of impressions gives place to another, but remains within
hailing distance. So it is here. The profaned ritual
remains at the back of the mind as we follow Oak home-
ward. The storm scenes in this novel have been admired
often, and justly, but we need to be fully aware of their

context. The episode gathers into itself both the country vocations and activities, and the tale of Bathsheba's bitter choice. 'Mr. Troy says it will not rain.' As Hardy describes Oak's perceptions of the oncoming storm we may discern in the prose a poignant appreciation of a kind of sensitiveness growing out of unison with the ways of nature, that he knows to be disappearing from contemporary life. The movements in the creature world, the life of toad and garden slug, have a strange magnitude. How sensuously, and how dramatically, the images and phrases record the moment when the shepherd strikes a light indoors, and then looks out again!

Even here, from time to time, there are lapses of manner, there are moments of forced sophistication. But as soon as Hardy becomes absorbed in his invention his distinction has free play, his prose recovers. Before the storm breaks we return to the revelry. The passage which frames the picture confronting Oak, abounds in quiet *double-entendres*. The meaning of the helpless, drunken farm folk, within the rhythm by now established, speaks for itself. But there are suggestive touches of imagery, too, like the presence of the evergreens with the burnt-down candles among them, or the hint of daily activities drawn from the look of the slumbering labourers. Oak's shout to one of the labourers draws all the strands together.

> 'Where's your thatching beetle and rick-stick and spars?'
> 'Under the staddles', said Moon, mechanically, with the unconscious promptness of a medium.

So the prelude ends, this movement between the barn of derision and the hut of understanding. A deliberate art is all the while preparing for the covering and thatching beneath the storm's menace, and the full dramatic significance of that storm appears only when it is

E

felt to complete a long episode. The general force, and the momentary stabbing effects, of the descriptive prose that follows, have often been appreciated. We are still dealing with an extreme pressure active just out of reach of the language it wants, and secure of its verbal effects only here and there. Hardy does feel deeply what the storm and the thatching and the shepherd's brave persistence signify. Strong impressions claim the attention, despite a muffled prose, and you cannot always account for them. The storm gains actuality from the recorded details of the labouring activities. Yet the basis of the writing is what it often is at these pressure points in a Hardy novel: stale literary reminiscence. Even that becomes vigorous: 'The night had a haggard look, like a sick thing.' At best there are touches as shrewd and impressive as 'A light flapped over the scene.' The true climax comes with a phrase of the first importance: ' . . . the darkness so intense that Gabriel worked entirely by feeling with his hands.'

The image constructed here must remind us of Clym working on the heath in his near-blindness; of Tess, toiling and faint, by the threshing machine at Flintcomb Ash. Oak in the darkness working with his hands is a radial point for all the perceptions about the storm and the farmstead. And still, as the scene develops, penetrating the fitful blur of literary veneer you have the vividly detected sound and shape etched suddenly upon the mind; and you hear voices, speaking sometimes with surprising poignancy, and reverberating strangely: 'I cannot find my husband. Is he with you?' Above all, gathering momentum with the tension of the story itself, there is everywhere the incessant activity. That reaches its own climax when the flash strikes the tree.

It sprang from east, west, north, south . . . dancing, leaping, striding, racing around . . .

In despite of an infuriated universe, a sort of response, indeed, to the fury itself, the thatching and the binding go on.

Now this is what the novel as a whole treats of. And Hardy's art is to engage this situation, in differing ways and with increasing profundity, in the best novels of the twenty years that followed. Oak in the storm is the beginning, and Tess with her friends at Flintcomb Ash is the culmination. The treatment of the theme gathers strength; and with such things as the Flintcomb Ash sequence in *Tess* we come to Hardy's most personal kind of achievement in fiction. Whatever may be the forces of antagonism, the thatching and the binding, the reaping and the stacking, go on. Value inheres in the persistence itself. Oak embodies that persistence. Oak, as he works with his hands in the darkness, blindly, becomes the strongest, clearest image for the steadfastness that, in his own person, he continually represents through the novel, whether in the story, or by his rôle in agricultural life.

The quality of the closing scenes is uneven. The bright, deceptive invader from the alien kingdom brings suffering both to Bathsheba and to Fanny, extreme suffering. Gradually, Bathsheba's country-bred stamina enables her to discover the full extent of her predicament. First, she turns to the country squire, and then, at last, to the shepherd-farmer; and she marries Oak.

THE RETURN OF THE NATIVE (1877–8)

THE country environment of *The Return of the Native* is not attractive, in the way that woods and farmlands and hills and fields are. The heath is formidably antagonistic to human society and human ways. This is the other side of the scene that dominates *Under the Greenwood Tree*, *Far from the Madding Crowd*, *The Trumpet-Major* and *The Wood-*

landers. But Egdon has an equally constructive function. Hardy includes the heath, not as a discord to be borne with, but as a conspiring element, permanently alongside farm and mill and dairy. In *Far from the Madding Crowd*, the storm was an episode, albeit a critical one. In *The Return of the Native*, the storm, in its character of antagonism, of dour hostility, seems to be present throughout. But it is a romantic and even a rather careless reading of the novel as a whole, that discovers simply a dualism, a dramatic conflict between the agricultural community and the heath. The heath does nourish this community; more, it nourishes the vitality, the purposeful staying-power, the continuing mirth, which sustain and are sustained by the community's labour. Hardy gives such weight to the hostile element in order to make our final appreciation of the agricultural reality more inclusive, more honest.

The famous sequence at the beginning of the novel, evoking the power and the presence of Egdon, gives a characteristic effect of hammering away at an intractable substance. It is not simply that Hardy is here trying to write impressively (though he is); much more, he is trying to reproduce a series of very deeply felt impressions which elude his command of language. There comes a moment of verification, when the pivot for the whole experience is revealed, in the person of a furze-cutter.

> Looking upwards, a furze-cutter would have been inclined to continue work; looking down, he would have decided to finish his faggot and go home.

After this, the heath is really about us, long-enduring, fecund, dour; so is the traditional style of agricultural life it has thrown up. Upon Egdon appear first the furze-cutter, then the Reddleman. The movement of thought and impulse behind their appearance culminates in an expressive visual structure, a shadowy group of village folk peopling the 'loftiest ground of the loneliest height that the heath contained'. The heath lights up with bonfires. Then,

> The first tall flame from Rainbarrow sprang into the sky. . . It seemed as if the bonfire-makers were standing in some radiant upper storey of the world, detached from and independent of the dark stretches below. . . . It was as if these men and boys had suddenly dived into past ages, and fetched therefrom an hour and deed which had before been familiar with this spot. . . . To light a fire is the instinctive and resistant act of man when, at the winter ingress, the curfew is sounded throughout Nature.

This age-old ritual of the village community, this ritual of spontaneous resistance to the dark fiat of nature, ends the movement that began with haggard and deserted Egdon. The brooding darkness of the heath, lit by the labourers' bonfires, repeats the crashing storm defied by Oak's persistence. The heath, it appears, nourishes the very vitality and stability it would threaten to destroy; and the vitality and the stability together penetrate the interchange of voices from which the tale itself now emerges.

The figure of Venn distinguishes *The Return of the Native* in a new way. The Reddleman seems to personify the interplay between the ballad-tale and the country environment that gives to Hardy's best novels their unique quality. Originally, Venn was to have no other function. 'He should disappear from the heath,' Hardy said, 'nobody knowing whither.' Then, in deference to his reading public, and to the fictional conventions he tacitly accepted, he connected the Reddleman more ordinarily with the conclusion of the tale. Venn seems not to belong to plot or character, as these are usually understood. He is like a chord, modulating between the heath and the fable. His craft, significantly, is a dying craft. 'Reddlemen are now but seldom seen.' Once, reddle used to colour all rural life thereabouts, challenging, as it were, the dark countenance of the heath. 'Reddle spreads its lively hues over everything it lights on.' The first account of Venn's trade is substantial, and his figure is so devised and used that, later on, every phrase regarding him flashes out towards a wider circuit of meaning. He exerts an odd fascination, for he is a particularly apt projection of Hardy's feeling for the country at this time: a man, so to speak, dyed into a way of life, and that way fast disappearing. At times, a dream-like quality enfolds him, a 'poetry of existence', suggesting an unchecked, regressive nostalgia in Hardy. But chiefly we feel in Venn those qualities of passive firmness, self-denying fidelity, and patient watchfulness, that Hardy values so much, and connects with the intimacies and the routines of agricultural life. His is not a day-dream figure; he is an effective emblem because Hardy represents him with detached accuracy as a particular practitioner of a particular trade. Local status defines his respectability, and his 'good nature' is allied to 'acuteness as extreme as it could be without verging on craft'. Venn suggests, in fact, simultaneously, a poetry of existence, and the finances of the trade in reddle.

The tale itself expresses the artist's meaning more directly than any other of Hardy's. His fictions are not as a rule so directly expressive; they may hold fast in the memory with their implications unresolved. Their imagery may be elusive. Illumination comes first from the contact between the tale and the country community. But in *The Return of the Native* the tale itself speaks clearly. The very grouping of the protagonists tells much. On one far side is Thomasin ('All similes concerning her began and ended with birds') and on the other, Wildeve, the ineffectual engineer, invading the country to become a publican. Clym (the native home from exile) and Eustacia (seeking exile, and confusing that with home) stand between them. At the centre, between Clym and Eustacia, Mrs. Yeobright is subtly placed, a countrywoman upholding urban attitudes whose true nature and effect she cannot perceive. (Mr. Melbury, in *The Woodlanders*, provides a more delicate study of the same kind.)

Clym himself is a key figure for a right appraisal of Hardy's art. He is the most direct representative of the novelist's strongest impulse in its simplest form: the return from town to country, and the rejection of urban life. Clym's experience never really includes the town or its world of thought: that menaces from beyond.

> An inner strenuousness was preying upon an outer symmetry. . . . He already showed that thought is a disease of flesh. . . . As for his look, it was a natural cheerfulness striving against depression from without. . . .

This early passage of exposition, constructed upon the dualism of natural mirth and the despair that invades from beyond agriculture, is important—the whole of it. Analysis is suspended while Clym walks across the dark heath. Hardy describes the journey with a warmth and a sensuous accuracy that move one deeply—it is a scene that develops the analysis with much richer art. Then, in the conversation between mother and son, flat, direct statement takes the place of imagery. There is no immediate answer to Clym's final question, 'Mother, what *is* doing well?' (The italics are the novelist's own.) But fundamentally, the novel at large takes up that kind of question, and the possibility of an answer.

The wholeheartedness of the native's return home is clear. '*Clym had been so inwoven with the heath in his boyhood. . . .*'

If anyone knew the heath well it was Clym. He was
permeated with its scenes, with its substance, and with its
odours. *He might be said to be its product.* . . . His estimate
of life had been coloured by it.

Clym's walk across the heath, and, still more, the later
scene in which the labourers feel their way over in pitch
darkness (like Oak, working with his hands in the night
of the storm) enlarge our sense of Hardy's meaning.
Oak's quiet perceptiveness, his intimacy with miniature
creature-life, first gave imaginative order to that meaning;
in *The Woodlanders*, a more uncanny intimacy provides the
finest image of all. Hardy writes of these movements
over Egdon, feeling, touching, smelling, sensing through
the darkness in a long-familiar way, so as to make you
feel that this intimacy has a value of its own. When
near-blindness overtakes Clym, his return home seems
absolute. Deflected from 'study', the source (as Hardy
found in his own experience) of 'despair from without',
he becomes perforce a furze cutter. By the end of the
story his desire to educate has been substantially modified.
Clym wants only to preach and teach the traditional
morality of Egdon.

Meanwhile, his near-blindness makes a peculiar metaphorical effect of its own. It prevents further study, and
denies any 'more perfect insight into the conditions of
existence.' At the same time it closes in the horizon,
as if to simplify the complexities of living. Together
with the more restricted field of vision there goes a more
thorough consciousness of the enclosed, vital area where
life still has meaning and mirth. The adjustment of this
imagined predicament to Hardy's bitter but profound
feeling makes possible a drily powerful nostalgic writing.
Here, for instance.

When in the full swing of labour, he was cheerfully disposed, and calm.

His daily life was of a curious microscopic sort, *his whole world being limited to a circuit of a few feet from his person*. His familiars were creeping and winged things. . . . Bees hummed about his ears with an intimate air, and tugged at the heath and furze-flowers at his side in such numbers as to weigh them down to the sod. The strange amber-coloured butterflies which Egdon produced. . . . quivered in the breath of his lips, alighted upon his bowed back, and sported with the glittering point of his hook as he flourished it up and down. Tribes of emerald-green grasshoppers leaped over his feet, falling awkwardly on their backs, heads, or hips, like unskilful acrobats. . . .

'Intimate' is the key-word. Hardy does not reach for the felicity of 'tugged'. Clym's microscopic world suggests it. But more, a special feeling towards this world leads out, through phrases such as 'which Egdon produced' and 'his bowed back', to the novel at large. That feeling pricks, suddenly, in the perception, 'quivered in the breath of his lips'; and 'the glittering point of his hook as he flourished it' with its reminder of the labouring activity, brings clearer definition. This particular passage falters where the quotation breaks off. Hardy seems to glance affectedly towards his readers. But whatever the unevenness, the long, affectionate record which includes the passage, sustains a power of its own. Flies, snakes, rabbits, inhabit this world, and the clinching sentence is 'None of them feared him.' He was frequently depressed in spirit, Hardy says, when not actually at work; cheerfully disposed and calm when in the full swing of labour. 'It was bitterly plain to Eustacia that he did not care much about social failure.' Such is the end of Clym's pilgrimage.

At a later point, the tale takes up these intimations, and echoes them. Mrs. Yeobright makes her journey to the hut on the heath, seeking to reconcile irreconcilables. She is a helpless, bewildered figure, confident that

tensions (as between town and country, between doing
well in her sense and doing well in Clym's) can be
resolved, when she has not grasped their nature. Her
journey, her despair and her death, make a moving narrative because of this, and one that has for background a
series of apprehensions of creature-life reflecting those of
Clym's daily living. Clym himself

> appeared of a russet hue, not more distinguishable from
> the scene around him than the green caterpillar from the leaf
> it feeds on. . . . The silent being who thus occupied himself
> seemed to be of no more account in life than an insect. He
> appeared as a mere parasite of the heath, fretting its surface
> in his daily labour as a moth frets a garment, entirely en-
> grossed with its products, having no knowledge of anything
> in the world but fern, furze, heath, lichens, and moss.

This seems to recapitulate the first long study of Clym's
new life. And the last paragraph of the chapter makes a
comparable effect, so felicitous in its imagery of detail,
and persistent in its references to the daily activities of
human life.

> The leaves of the hollyhocks hung like half-closed um-
> brellas, the sap almost simmered in the stems. . . .

The microscopic, thriving life of the heath is continually vivid as Mrs. Yeobright journeys away from the
hut. There is the affecting last conversation with the
young boy. When he has gone,

> . . . all visible animation disappeared from the landscape,
> though the intermittent husky notes of the male grass-
> hoppers from every tuft of furze were enough to show that
> amid the prostration of the larger animal species *an unseen
> insect world was busy in all the fulness of life*.

The fecundity persists, a microcosm of the rural home.
Eustacia's dream of escape from that home never
seems to be other than a dream. The chapter describing

her, near the beginning of the novel, hardly deserves the kind of praise it has received. She does not convince, except as a silent presence, threatening security. Like Thomasin, she belongs to a madrigal; but she has not about her the details of living and working. She is the phantom, the queen of the night. We take her fascination on trust, unless it is the labourer Charley who convinces us of it. The seclusion of the country community breeds the longing to break away, and the longing breeds the enticing dream. But how blurred the dream is: its slight validity collapses when sensuous impressions of the bank, the barrow, the pool and the furze patch, collect alongside it.

Fortunately, the general force of the conception carries the reader past many weaknesses. The story's irony is compelling, and its setting gives rich meaning to it. The deeply-rooted communal life expresses itself in the bonfire ritual and the wedding rejoicings, in the mumming, and the fair, and the effigy. The Reddleman seems in some measure to personify it. The deep source of this life of the heath hamlets is in dark and fecund Egdon itself; and it will persist, through whatever catastrophe, numbed, but strong.

THE MAYOR OF CASTERBRIDGE (1884–5)

The Mayor of Casterbridge relates closely to *The Return of the Native*. The one is dominated by a heath, the other by a person, each expressing the harsher aspect of agricultural life. Oak has darkened into Henchard, and the market town of Weatherbury into Egdon Heath. Here, nothing is seen under an ideal light: *The Mayor of Casterbridge* acknowledges the bitter situation of agriculture in contemporary England. Henchard suffers defeat, and passes, and the village rites pass with him: the tolling of the bell, consecrated burial, and the tending of the grave. Casterbridge is an image of Dorchester, the nearby town of Hardy's youth, and his presentation of it derives from local recollection, a turning from the precarious present back to a stable past.

Henchard suggests a vitality, an instinctive and commanding zest, which call in question our usual assessments of human worth. He is the most Lawrentian of Hardy's figures. The novel nowhere elucidates the valuable elements in Henchard's nature; his worth is taken for granted, it seems, bound up though it is with obduracy, arrogance, blindness. The whole-hearted commitment to a satisfying way of life, the virile warmth and generosity of spirit, the dogged courage, are the more effective for being left unstressed.

> During the day Farfrae learnt from the men that Henchard had kept Abel's old mother in coals and snuff all the previous winter, which made him less antagonistic to the corn-factor.

That occurs at the moment of Henchard's first downfall in Casterbridge. On the other hand, he is spared nothing. The novel's impact comes of a confidence that the qualities Henchard incarnates have more than personal roots, and will survive the personal and transitory degradations. With this man for subject, even the more conventionally literary gestures succeed. 'He rose to his feet and stood like a dark ruin.'

The success originates in the conviction with which the mayor is present as a member of his community. His voice, for instance, emerges from among other voices:

> 'With all my heart', said the first fiddle. 'We've let back our strings, that's true; but we can soon pull 'em up again. Sound A, neighbours, and give the man a stave.'
> 'I don't care a curse what the words be,' said Henchard. 'Hymns, ballets, or rantipole rubbish; the Rogue's March

or the cherubim's warble—'tis all the same to me if 'tis good harmony, and well put out.'

'Well—heh, heh—it may be we can do that, and not a man among us that have sat in the gallery less than twenty year. . . .'

It is speech (and the talk is superb in parts of this novel) with the life and activities of a close-knit community behind it. The quality of Henchard's voice brings the whole personality before us:

'Chuck across one of your psalters—Old Wiltshire is the only tune worth singing—the psalm-tune that would make my blood ebb and flow like the sea when I was a steady chap.'

The thrust is irresistible; the phrases transcend their context.

'I'll find some words to fit 'en. . . . 'Od seize your sauce —I tell ye to sing the Hundred-and-Ninth, to Wiltshire, and sing it you shall! . . . Not a single one of all the droning crew of ye goes out of this room till that Psalm is sung! . . .'

He belongs to a labouring community no more sentimentalized than he is himself. And his story, too, is a strong, ironic conception, and it enacts forcefully the tension between the old rural world and the new urban one. Farfrae is the invader, the stranger within the gates. The novelist regards him with detachment and some insight, but as an alien. The continuous irony is a local manifestation of a general vigour. It is an obvious irony, a thread easy to follow, one of the traditional arts of the balladist that came to Hardy almost instinctively.

The Mayor of Casterbridge, then, is the tale of the struggle between the native countryman and the alien invader; of the defeat of dull courage and traditional attitudes by insight, craft, and the vicissitudes of nature; and of the persistence through that defeat of some deep layer of vitality in the country protagonist. It is a mistake to think of Hardy as mixing together ingredients like plot, design, irony, and character-drawing. We need to think, rather, of the ways in which all that Henchard represents makes itself felt in the whole texture to which irony and character and design contribute.

Casterbridge and its folk and the feeling for the community's life come first. The market town of the past has its origin in the needs of agriculture. 'Casterbridge was the complement of the rural life around; not its urban opposite.'

> Casterbridge was in most respects but the pole, focus, or nerve-knot of the surrounding country life; differing from the many manufacturing towns which are as foreign bodies set down, like boulders on a plain, in a green world with which they have nothing in common.

But the guiding assertions depend upon moments of imaginative invention, like this one.

> And in autumn airy spheres of thistledown floated into the same street, lodged upon the shop-fronts, blew into drains; and innumerable tawny and yellow leaves skimmed along the pavement, and stole through people's doorways into their passages, with a hesitating scratch on the floor, like the skirts of timid visitors.

The movement of this prose is supple and easy; the turns of phrase spring from precision of feeling. There is a lovely affection about the close, with its characteristic reference to human doings. The visitors in passages are present in the same moment of experience with the leaves that betoken the surrounding country. In a similar way, Casterbridge is first identified by its shop windows as they appear to two strangers.

> Scythes, reap-hooks, sheep-shears, bill-hooks, spades, mattocks, and hoes at the ironmonger's; beehives, butter-

firkins, churns, milking stools and pails, hay-rakes, field-flagons, and seed-lips at the cooper's; cart-ropes and plough harness at the saddler's. . . . .

and so on. The shops of the township are filled with the implements of agriculture. Again,

> The corn grown on the upland side of the borough was garnered by farmers who lived in an eastern purlieu called Durnover. Here wheat-ricks overhung the old Roman street, and thrust their eaves against the church tower; green-thatched barns . . . opened directly upon the main thoroughfare. . . . Here lived burgesses who daily walked the fallow; shepherds in an intra-mural squeeze. A street of farmers' homesteads—a street ruled by a mayor and corporation, yet echoing with the thump of the flail, the flutter of the winnowing fan, and the purr of milk into the pails. . . .

Henchard, the mayor, takes his actuality from this wealth of perceived detail. The writing is beset with buying and selling, the reaping and garnering of corn, and the activities and movements of profitable labour.

The common folk of Casterbridge make another contribution. In the earlier novels, whether by allusion, by report of events, or by conversation, the old village traditions and rituals strike the reader as little climaxes: the bonfire, the shearing supper. Here, our sense is of men going about their daily affairs, the flurry, the chatter, the sights and sounds. The workmen and the communities of Mixen Lane and 'The Three Mariners' are Hardy's best achievement in this vein, and they count for more than the rustics of the other novels. Vivid memories inform the treatment, and colour the expressive, colloquial voices. But the treatment is dry, unsparing. Theirs are the voices which vouch for Henchard, and so for the novel. The fine passage when the mayor's curse

emerges out of the inarticulate affability of the inn will
be remembered. A subtler and more sustained passage
describes the arrival of Farfrae, and his first evening at the
inn. There is a sort of gaiety about Hardy's irony here;
but some of the labourers' speech makes an effect not
far from poignancy. When Farfrae sings his emotional
and alien song of longing for home, the company is taken
unawares. They can hardly conceive of any balladry
or music less direct and forthright in its convention than
their own.

> 'What did ye come away from yer own country for,
> young maister, if ye be so wownded about it?' inquired
> Christopher Coney, from the background. . . . 'Faith, it
> wasn't worth your while on our account, for, as Maister
> Billy Wills says, we be bruckle folk here—the best o' us
> hardly honest sometimes, what with hard winters, and so
> many mouths to fill, and God-a'mighty sending his little
> taties so terrible small to fill 'em with. . . .'

They are baffled that a man should sing so truthlessly.
And the idiomatic terms bring to bear upon both singer
and song a crumpling vigour. Yet that vigour convinces
through, not in spite of or in ignorance of, the more
mean and sordid aspects of the community's life. If
there is nostalgia here, it is strangely without illusions.
But there are the usual hints of the sheltered and shut-in
group. Scotland, like Bath in *Far from the Madding
Crowd*, is foreign, is infinitely remote; and the rough
touches of caricature tell us that Hardy has to control
disordered feelings.

The vigour and colloquial strength of this little community of voices becomes more personal in the speech
of figures such as Mrs. Cuxsom, Abel Whittle, and the
furmity woman, more personal still in Henchard himself. The first voice heard in Casterbridge has the tonic
quality.

'You must be a real stranger here not to know what's made all the poor volks' insides plim like blowed bladders this week?'

All the voices have it.

'And as for he—well, there—(lowering her voice) 'tis said 'a was a poor parish 'prentice . . . that began life wi' no more belonging to 'en than a carrion crow. . . .'

'Ah, yes, Cuxsom's gone, and so shall leather breeches! . . .'

''Twas that that kept us so low upon ground—that great hungry family.'

'Ay. Where the pigs be many the wash runs thin.'

'And dostn't mind how mother would sing, Christopher?' continued Mrs. Cuxsom. . . . 'and how we went with her to the party at Mellstock, do ye mind?—at old Dame Ledlow's, farmer Shinar's aunt, do ye mind?—she we used to call Toadskin, because her face was so yaller and freckled, do ye mind?'

To make the excerpt is to spoil it; but only so shall we notice how incessant are the little references to the detail of village life. That last passage of memories ends with music, music and dance, and it seems to go to the heart of this special social mirth. The phraseology is stylized, the rhythm remains personal (but for the Shakespearian echoes) and the idiom of the whole is sharp with memories. Hardy succeeds, in fact, with every aspect of Casterbridge life, at the bridge, in Mixen Lane, during the Skimmity Ride, inside the homes.

'And she was white as marble-stone,' said Mrs. Cuxsom. 'And likewise such a thoughtful woman, too—ah, poor soul —that 'a minded every little thing that wanted tending. . . .'

Mrs. Cuxsom's elegy is one of Hardy's loveliest achievements, and deservedly known and praised. There is no need to quote it again. The interruptions, touched with parody, seem to add power to it, a superb invention of

F

the village voice turning over the details of village life. That the moment so heightened in feeling (like the conversation quoted above) should be elegiac, is not surprising.

> 'Well, poor soul; she's helpless to hinder that or anything now,' answered Mother Cuxsom. 'And all her shining keys will be took from her, and her cupboards opened; and little things 'a didn't wish seen, anybody will see; and her wishes and ways will all be as nothing.'

'Why, save the man', remarks an anonymous voice at the very beginning of the novel,

> 'What wisdom's in him, that 'a should come to Weydon for a job of that sort this time o' year? . . . Pulling down is more the nater of Weydon. There were five houses cleared away last year, and three this; and the volk nowhere to go— no, not so much as a thatched hurdle; that's the way o' Weydon-Priors.

We must not be dull to these implications, if we would enter into the meaning of Hardy's fiction. *The Mayor of Casterbridge* turns on the situation that led to the repeal of the Corn Laws. The consequences of that repeal to Victorian agricultural life are the centre of this book, provide the impulse that makes it what it is. The note sounded by that first voice is resumed in the quiet footnote of a later page: 'These chimes, like those of many country Churches, have been silenced for many years.'

THE WOODLANDERS (1885–7)

The Woodlanders is the novel that most comprehensively expresses Hardy's feeling towards agricultural life, and his sense of its resistance to despair. It is his most fluid book; the talk and the activities of the lesser country folk are joined into the rhythm of the whole, and not contrived as an episodic chorus or commentary. The writing finds and states its objects with more confidence; the writer, one feels, is clearer in his own mind about his personal predicament. 'It was one of those sequestered spots outside the gates of the world', he begins. And when that spring is released again, later in the story, you feel something like exultancy in the nostalgia.

> Day after day waxed and waned; the one or two woodmen who sawed, shaped, or spokeshaved on her father's premises at this inactive season of the year, regularly came and unlocked the doors in the morning, locked them in the evening, supped, leant over their garden-gates for a whiff of evening air, and to catch any last and furthest throb of news from the outer world, which entered and expired at Little Hintock like the exhausted swell of a wave in some innermost cavern of some innermost creek of an embayed sea. . .

Like *Far from the Madding Crowd*, the tale tells of the choice between agricultural life and the lure of the town, the lure of 'rising in the world', confronting a country girl; and the outcome of the story embodies imaginatively the implications of the choice made. Grace Melbury is a second Bathsheba, a quieter, subtler study, less vividly drawn, but drawn with a rather deeper respect for human complexity. Giles Winterbourne re-enacts the function of Gabriel Oak, while Marty South resumes Venn's function. In her the resilient local community takes personal form and skill. She is 'rooted in one dear perpetual place' and she disengages herself at the end from the individual lives and destinies of the surviving protagonists, and—so to say—simply continues to be. Egdon was a darker image of the rural environment than the hillsides and farms of Weatherbury; now in the woods of *The Woodlanders* Weatherbury and Egdon seem to fuse together, the open loveliness and the bounty of the first, and the overshadowing presence so intimately declared, and the inner fecundity, of the second. In *The Return of the Native* every insect and creature is alive, stirs, troubles the eye. In *The Woodlanders* every footfall crushes leaves, every touch and smell is of twigs and trees. Moreover the woods combine suggestions of long generations, of near-agelessness, with particular moments in the community's past (when this plantation was made, when the great gale blew). And they continually remind us of human cultivation, human participation in the slow work of time.

But in one important particular this tale of choice stands apart from the earlier ones. Bathsheba finally chose the agricultural order and married Oak. When Winterborne, in *The Woodlanders*, the representative woodman, dies, Grace fulfils her father's social ambition and accepts the rôle she has been trained for. A diminished person, she returns to Fitzpiers; and Hardy lays firm but varied stress upon that choice as an issue of life-commitment. He also made it clear, in private comment, that he envisaged no happiness for her. *Far from the Madding Crowd* reflects through its fable turbulence and insecurity, but *The Woodlanders* reflects defeat. The last voice in the novel is Marty's, and a lonely devotion and loyalty speak in one who incarnates the finest part of country attitudes. Grace has turned to Fitzpiers, a Fitzpiers who has made the accommodating gesture (and how revealing a gesture!) of renouncing his studies. Marty takes Venn's place. What was projected before in the active, resilient practitioner of a dying trade, is projected now in the strong-willed, but lonely, impotent mourner, who polishes a dead man's tools and tends his grave. A richer, more personal and truthful apprehension underlies the second figure.

Fitzpiers' renunciation takes its origin from a more

obvious kind of honesty in Hardy. He knew well where studies of that kind led. At this very time of his life he himself was renewing his efforts to master German metaphysics. Studies were the heart of his experience of the 'outer' world. But such a renunciation is, of course, no way of dealing with the situation; it is a gesture of despair, of abandonment. And this is not like the despair of the countryman, which does not stunt the pursuit of activity, even vain activity. Grace makes the paralysing choice, and (as in *The Mayor of Casterbridge*) the future seems to offer no happiness or resolution. In Clym's last vocation and Venn's trade, in the life and death of the Mayor, you have the feeling that theirs is a dying way of life. Now, in the union of Grace and Fitzpiers after the death of Giles, the feeling gets clearer definition. This story deals more subtly than its predecessors with personal and social relations, at some sacrifice of the sharp, hard edges of the character-drawing in the other books. Social status is integral to the pattern of the story; its protagonists each love 'above' himself or herself. That, too, indicates one facet of the impending collapse of the closed, compact agricultural communities. There are passages in *The Woodlanders*, however, where Hardy stands aside from his invention in a new way, and provides a troubled, intrusive commentary, one that speaks for the despair from outside, not the despair of the country which is able to endure patiently and hope on. It seeps into the movement of the novel. In the phrase of Mr. Eliot, the man who suffers is less well separated from the mind that creates. Canalized nostalgia gives place, occasionally, to a coarser indulgence of bitterness.

But we find here some of Hardy's finest things. Marty South is perhaps the most moving of his characters, and two special reasons for the success suggest themselves.

First, she is constantly present in scenes of activity and skill, sharpening spars, or planting young trees. Second, her speaking is often contrived with lovely imaginative truth, and a very personal movement. 'Her face', Hardy says,

> had the usual fulness of expression which is developed by a life of solitude. Where the eyes of a multitude continuously beat like waves upon a countenance they seem to wear away its mobile power; but in the still water of privacy, every feeling and sentiment unfolds in visible luxuriance. . . .

'Mobile', it would be. Serenity and happiness seem to exist, for Hardy, in consonant and harmonious activities. Notice, too, how the solitude of seclusion from the urban world conditions the natural expressiveness. This 'still water of privacy' must remind us of 'sequestered spots' and the 'embayed sea': that note is insistent.

But the figure of Marty is no simple invention. A daydream character, you think. The wonderful hair, though it may help to express the physical fineness of the country girl, completes the daydream quality. Then she is robbed of her claim to comeliness, and robbed in order to add a biting touch of falsity to Mrs. Charmond, the invader, the bewitching visitor in the agricultural group. And in fact, wherever Marty moves and speaks and works, as the novel develops, you become aware of a valuable mode of living. Hardy makes his most moving effects with just an air of adding corroboratory detail. He is absorbed in his object.

> 'It will be fine to-morrow,' said Marty, observing them with the vermilion light of the sun in the pupils of her eyes, 'for they are a-croupied down nearly at the end of the bough.'

> Marty South was an adept at peeling the upper parts; and there she stood encaged amid the mass of twigs and buds like a great bird, running her ripping tool into the smallest

branches, beyond the furthest points to which the skill and patience of the men enabled them to proceed. . . .

'You seem to have a better instrument than they, Marty', said Fitzpiers.

'No, sir,' she said, holding up the tool, a horse's leg-bone fitted into a handle and filed to an edge; ''tis only that they've less patience with the twigs, because their time is worth more than mine.'

Hardy's appraisal of the worth of agricultural life is never far removed from his appreciation of agricultural economics.

Marty South embodies, then, a wholly fresh expression of Hardy's intelligent appraisal of the human possibilities of this way of life, with all its limitations. An ideal figure, we may say; but Hardy does present her, with conscious art, precisely as that. She brings to dramatic life, out of her close involvement in each facet of the novel, one possibility of meaning and worth. Her plain dignity, quite without pretension, defines one element of potential good inherent in the Little Hintock world, a good that matters even more than a single life, or two lives, spent and lost in affirming and celebrating it. There is tenderness in the way Hardy presents her, and there is more than a hint of nostalgia. But the language that brings her to life is careful and never false. She cuts spars with blistered hands. She is hired out for her living.

Is it possible to be more explicit about this 'good'? In part, certainly, it consists in intimacy with the plenitude of the natural order. We perceive it in the descriptions of Oak before and after the storm, of Clym at night upon Egdon and by day among the furze. Here is an illuminating passage.

The casual glimpses which the ordinary population bestowed upon that wondrous world of sap and leaves called the Hintock woods, had been with these two, Giles and Marty, a clear gaze. They had been possessed of its finer mysteries as of commonplace knowledge; had been able to read its hieroglyphs as ordinary writing; to them the sights and sounds of night, winter, wind, storm, amid those dense boughs, which had to Grace a touch of the uncanny, and even of the supernatural, were simple occurrences, whose origin, continuance, and laws they foreknew. They had planted together, and together they had felled; together they had, with the run of the years, mentally collected those remoter signs and symbols which seen in few were of runic obscurity, but all together made an alphabet. From the light lashing of the twigs upon their faces when brushing through them in the dark, they could pronounce upon the species of tree whence they stretched; from the quality of the wind's murmur through a bough, they could in like manner name its sort afar off. They knew by a glance at a trunk if its heart were sound, or tainted with incipient decay; and by the state of its upper twigs the stratum that had been reached by its roots. The artifices of the seasons were seen by them from the conjuror's own point of view, and not from that of the spectator.

The unevenness of this passage makes it less than fairly representative of *The Woodlanders*; but it is uneven in illuminating ways. As you read the opening sentences, the prose seems like a laboured translation out of another language, and the trite handling of words is quite disconcerting. Periphrasis masquerades as impressiveness, the repetition is trying. Yet the very laboriousness has to do with an integrity the mannerisms would deny. With *To them, the sights and sounds* . . . the fluency of the movement and the solemnity of the cadence give you pause; Hardy is not always most trustworthy when most fluent. Then the odd phrase *mentally collected* jars the attention. Here is Hardy's sort of vigour, the elusive thing tightly gripped, at whatever cost in suavity. The earnest emphatic manner reappears, and then suddenly, with *From the light lashing of the twigs* . . . the intended movement is under way. Statement is left behind, and the perceptions act out the insight; and with this language of perceptions Hardy can speak like a master. Even then, he falters again, turns to his reader and explains—with a false analogy. Then see how beautifully he recovers his poise, with Marty's voice.

> 'He ought to have married you, Marty, and nobody else in the world!' . . . .
> Marty shook her head. 'In all our outdoor days and years together, ma'am,' she replied, 'the one thing he never spoke of to me was love; nor I to him.'
> 'Yet you and he could speak in a tongue that nobody else knew—not even my father, though he came nearest knowing —the tongue of the trees and fruits and flowers themselves.'

Grace's reply is serious and sincere, yet laboured. But Marty's effort to sound a responsive note of adequate dignity gives a human implication to the experience of sensitive harmony with woodland life. Consider the delicacy of those words 'outdoor days', how they at once separate Marty from Giles, and bring them together not as lovers but as labourers. Then the gently deferential 'ma'am' reminds us of what now divides the two women also: the tragic marriage, and the way things have gone. Continually, in ways like this, Hardy has the delicate adjustment of individuals to local life and work issue in an equivalent delicacy of human feeling and relationship. You feel this quality in some measure whenever the woods come to life in the narrative, their sights and sounds, their growth and abundance, and whenever the novelist records intimations of the life and uniqueness of the trees.

A lingering wind brought to her ear the creaking sound of two overcrowded branches . . . which were rubbing each other into wounds, and other vocalized sorrows of the trees, together with the screech of owls, and the fluttering tumble of some awkward wood-pigeon ill-balanced on its roosting-bough.

True, the sense of intimacy sometimes proves a temptation to that intrusive commentary I have mentioned.

Here, as everywhere, the Unfulfilled Intention, which makes life what it is, was as obvious as it could be among the depraved crowds of a city slum. The leaf was deformed, the curve was crippled, the taper was interrupted; the lichen ate the vigour of the stalk, and the ivy slowly strangled to death the promising sapling.

But such passages suggest also the honesty with which Hardy wanted to assess the country consolation. The insights he brings from outside probe at the sheltered world and give to the prose a shabby violence. Something of the kind happens whenever Hardy seeks to come to terms artistically with complexities his art as a novelist is insufficient to focus. For the most part of the book, he expresses something quite different.

The holes were already dug, and they set to work. Winterborne's fingers were endowed with a gentle conjuror's touch in spreading the roots of each little tree, resulting in a sort of caress under which the delicate fibres all laid themselves out in their proper directions for growth. He put most of these roots towards the south-west; for, he said, in forty years' time, when some great gale is blowing from that quarter, the trees will require the strongest hold-fast on that side to stand against it and not fall.

'How they sigh directly we put 'em upright, though while they're lying down they don't sigh at all,' said Marty.

'Do they?' said Giles. 'I've never noticed it.'

She erected one of the young pines into its hole, and held

up her finger; the soft musical breathing instantly set in, which was not to cease night or day till the grown tree should be felled.

The feeling is for growth, for life. And its intimate quality is inseparable from the activities and skills of woodland living. The novel is not a collection of private descriptive set pieces; they have dramatic validity. The feeling towards the woods wells up from within the frame of the narrative.

The scene of the gathering around the woodfire after the bark-ripping, in chapter XIX, is a fine illustration. It forms an image at a point of rest, where the themes of the novel gather.

> Melbury mounted on the other side, and they drove on out of the grove, their wheels silently crushing delicate-patterned mosses, hyacinths, primroses, lords-and-ladies, and other strange and common plants, and cracking up little sticks that lay across the track. Their way homeward ran along the western flank of Dogbury Hill. . . .
>
> It was the cider country, which met the woodland district on the sides of this hill. . . . Under the blue, the orchards were in a blaze of pink bloom. . . . At a gate, which opened down the incline, a man leant on his arms, regarding this fair promise so intently that he did not observe their passing.
>
> 'That was Giles,' said Melbury, when they had gone by.
>
> 'Was it? Poor Giles,' said she.
>
> 'All that apple-blooth means heavy autumn work for him and his hands. If no blight happens before the setting, the cider yield will be such as we have not had for years.'

Grace has hitherto been poised uncertainly between Winterborne and Fitzpiers. Now she leaves the firelit circle where the human and social implications of her impending choice became so clear. Her father is carrying her away; the wheels of the gig crush the miniature world of green growth. They glimpse a distant Winterborne gazing out, absorbed, upon the tokens of abundant apple harvest. They are separated by their separate commitments, he to cultivation and the returning seasons of Hintock, she to her father's social ambition and the fruition of her civic and 'foreign' education. Dully she sets the yeoman aside. 'Was it? Poor Giles.' Her choice numbs her sensitiveness. Her loss of interest in and intimacy with the world of undergrowth and apple harvest becomes a withdrawal of personal warmth. But her father's deepest commitment is still to Hintock: this is part of the suggestive force of that promise to the dead father which still binds him to the son. He sees the yeoman, and feels the bond which unites them. Alongside the waste and pathos implied by the girl's curt dismissal, he brings into play feelings of a contrary order. The seasonal plenitude of earth and tree, and the labour which is the human response to it, these will persist.

The relation with the natural agricultural order which Hardy brings to life, reflects itself in many ways, but especially in the conduct of personal relations. Sensitiveness to people is an echo of a person's sensitiveness in the rural order. At one extreme is Mrs. Charmond.

> As a rule she takes no interest in the village folk at all . . .
> she's been used to such a wonderful life, and finds it dull here.

Of her it is curtly noted—'hardly knowing a beech from a woak.' Marty is at the other extreme, alert as even Giles is not, hearing the sound the young trees set up. Consider how the connection of that intimacy with degrees of human sensitiveness declares itself as that very passage continues.

> 'It seems to me,' the girl continued, 'as if they sigh because they are very sorry to begin life in earnest—just as we be.'

'Just as we be?' He looked critically at her. 'You ought not to feel like that, Marty.'

Her only reply was turning to take up the next tree; and they planted on through a great part of the day, almost without another word. Winterborne's mind ran on his contemplated evening party, his abstraction being such that he hardly was conscious of Marty's presence beside him.

From the nature of their employment, in which he handled the spade and she merely held the tree, it followed that he got good exercise and she got none. But she was a heroic girl, and though her outstretched hand was chill as a stone, and her cheeks blue, and her cold worse than ever, she would not complain whilst he was disposed to continue work. But when he paused she said, 'Mr. Winterborne, can I run down the lane and back to warm my feet?'

'Why, yes, of course,' he said, awakening to her existence. 'Though I was just thinking what a mild day it is for the season. Now I warrant that cold of yours is twice as bad as it was. You had no business to chop that hair off, Marty; it serves you almost right.'

This quiet-voiced ironical commentary upon their differing sensitiveness is well-judged. One flinches at the callousness of the concluding remarks, and though that callousness is unconscious, Giles is found wanting.

There is a richer passage earlier, where Giles awaits Grace's homecoming, in Sherton Abbas—her return to the country. He has been sent by Melbury, and stands watching for her. For the very beginning of the episode Hardy has worked in a metaphorical way, as Melbury saw Giles out of sight. When the actual encounter comes, the metaphorical quality is plain and vivid.

Standing, as he always did, at this season of the year, with his specimen apple tree in the midst, the boughs rose above the heads of the farmers, and brought a delightful suggestion of orchards into the heart of the town.

When her eye fell upon him for the last time he was
standing somewhat apart, holding the tree like an ensign. . . .

While she regarded him, he lifted his eyes in a direction
away from Marty and his face kindled with recognition and
surprise. She followed his gaze, and saw . . . Miss Grace
Melbury, but now looking glorified and refined to much
above her former level. Winterborne, *being fixed to the spot
by his apple tree, could not advance to meet her:* he held out his
spare hand with his hat in it, and with some embarrassment
beheld her coming on tiptoe through the mud to the middle
of the square where he stood . . . the little look of shame-
facedness she showed at having to perform the meeting with
him under an apple-tree ten feet high in the middle of the
market-place.

The verve of the imagery displaying the encounter is
naïve and delightful: Giles with his ensign, the tree;
Giles turning away from Marty; Giles unable to move
towards the glorified and refined Grace because of the
tree—although there is no subtlety, phrase after phrase
proves touchingly suggestive. Then the quality of the
personal relations comes out more evidently, and what
those relations imply.

'Don't Brownley's farm-buildings look strange to you,
now they have been moved bodily from the hollow where
the old ones stood to the top of the hill?' . . . .

'They had a good crop of bittersweets, they couldn't
grind them all'—nodding towards an orchard where some
heaps of apples had been left lying ever since the ingathering.

She said 'Yes,' but looking at another orchard.

'Why, you are looking at John-apple trees! You know
bittersweets—you used to well enough?'

'I am afraid I have forgotten, and it is getting too dark
to distinguish.'

Hardy spares Grace nothing of the consequences of that
darkness. The nerve of her insensitiveness to Giles and
to Giles's world has been touched. It was getting too

dark to distinguish. We recall an earlier colloquy. Mr. Melbury had prepared Giles.

'We, living here alone, don't notice how the whitey brown creeps out of the earth over us; but she, fresh from a city—why, she'll notice everything!'

'That she will,' said Giles.

Giles may be said to stand in somewhat the same relation to Grace—the real Grace—as Marty towards himself. But Giles is a woodlander, a protagonist in the story, and before us more often; so while Marty represents an ideal possibility beyond him, Giles in practice represents the worth of the agricultural life and skills and the worthiness of the traditional virtues—chivalry, loyalty, devotion. His symbolic function shows clearly at certain points in the novel; once or twice the feeling towards him is almost anthropological. There is first the passage where he stands with his apple tree in the market place. Then this:

An apple-mill and press had been erected on the spot, to which some men were bringing fruit from divers points in mawn-baskets, while others were grinding them, and others wringing down the pomace, whose sweet juice gushed forth into tubs and pails. The superintendent . . . was a young yeoman. . . . He had hung his coat to a nail of the outhouse wall, and wore his shirt-sleeves rolled up beyond his elbows to keep them unstained while he rammed the pomace into the bags of horsehair. Fragments of apple-rind had alighted upon the brim of his hat—probably from the bursting of a bag—while brown pips of the same fruit were sticking among the down upon his fine round arms, and in his beard.

It is much more than picturesque. Giles is not a day-dream figure. The whole context is rich with sensuous and mobile suggestion. A virile pleasure in the activities directs the nostalgic emotion: the verbs and participles make the effect—*grinding, wringing, gushed, rammed, sticking*. Then, much later in the tale, comes a third construction:

> Winterborne walked by her side in the rear of the apple-mill. He looked and smelt like Autumn's very brother, his face being sunburnt to a wheat-colour, his eyes blue as cornflowers, his sleeves and leggings dyed with fruit-stains, his hands clammy with the sweet juice of apples, his hat sprinkled with pips, and everywhere about him that atmosphere of cider which at its first return each season has such an indescribable fascination for those who have been born and bred among the orchards.

This remarkable passage forms part of the prolonged study of Grace's restoration, one of the finest sequences in the book. (This restoration, by a new immersion in agricultural life, cleansing, refreshing, and renewing resource for living, is woven into the texture of each of Hardy's major novels. Bathsheba, Clym, and Grace all experience it; so, once, and then again, in a harsher way, does Tess.) The sensuousness here is more vital than before, and the range of suggestion—*wheat colour*, *blue as cornflowers*, *dyed with fruit-stains*, *return each season*, *orchards*—is wider.

When Giles dies, the loss is communal. Marty's elegy for him is well known; Creedle's speech is important too.

> 'Forgive me, but I can't rule my mourning nohow as a man should, Mr. Melbury,' he said. 'I ha'n't seen him since Thursday se'night, and ha' wondered for days and days where he's been keeping. There was I expecting him to come and tell me to wash out the cider barrels against the making, and here was he. . . . Well, I've knowed him from table-high; I knowed his father—used to bide about up on two sticks in the sun afore he died!—and now I've seen the end of the family which we can ill afford to lose, wi' such a scanty lot o' good folk in Hintock as we've got. And now Robert Creedle will be nailed up in parish boards a' b'lieve; and nobody will glutch down a sigh for he!'

Hardy uses the local idiomatic word with restraint: when he brings it in, it carries special force. Creedle gives us a sense of the interdependence of the labouring lives in Hintock, and of solicitude for old age. Hardy works close to the economic grain of this labouring life. The haunting figure of old South, for instance, identifies the close connection between the labourer's livelihood and provision for the future, and the tenure of land and home. The chapters that present him, XII to XIV, belong to Hardy's own realm of narrative art: he is a ballad figure accommodated in fiction, whose bizarre impotence gives a nightmare shape to Hardy's darker apprehensions. His obsessions turn upon tenure and the tree's life is his life.

Indeed the whole tale turns upon these issues, and upon the power so to dissolve old local ties and commitments now vested in the mildly, stupidly predatory figure of Mrs. Charmond, the interloper. Marty is deprived. Giles is made dependent upon the representative of the new and alien squirearchy, and loses his home. These are the mainsprings of the fable. When Giles becomes a wanderer, Hardy drives home the gravity of the predicament. (Both the use of Mrs. Charmond in this context, and the theme of deprivation, look forward to the alien squire of *Tess of the D'Urbervilles*, and the homeless plight of the family at the end of that novel.)

> Winterborne walked up and down his garden next day thinking of the contingency. The sense that the paths he was pacing, the cabbage plots, the apple-trees, his dwelling, cider-cellar, wring-house, stables, weathercock, were all slipping away over his head and beneath his feet as if they were painted on a magic-lantern slide, was curious. . . .

When he returns to his home later, a visitor in the twilight, the shapes of things past discernible in the gloom, and the unharvested apples, speak eloquently. And when

G

Mrs. Charmond's carriage crashes into the ruins of Giles's cottage and overturns, the narrative assumes vivid poetic force. Quite evidently the whole episode engaged Hardy's most powerful feelings.

Finally, Giles stands for traditional agricultural codes of conduct, and these codes too have their part in the 'good' which *The Woodlanders* seeks to embody. Ponderously, at one point, Hardy stresses his intention.

> The wrong, the social sin, of now taking advantage of the offer of her lips, had a magnitude in the eyes of one whose life had been so primitive, so ruled by household laws, as Giles's, which can hardly be explained.

The conviction is real; and the tenderness with which Hardy treats of Giles in the final chapters flowers from this conviction. 'Her timid morality had indeed under-rated his chivalry.' Thus Grace is criticized; and the chivalry by which she is judged has its origin not in 'Victorian morality' but in customs of behaviour sanctioned by immemorial household laws of village communities.

I have tried to express something of the body behind such a phrase as 'He looked and smelt like Autumn's very brother.' Let us now consider Grace Melbury a little further. Bathsheba was most impressive in repentance and restoration. For Grace, no such complete restoration is possible, but Hardy feels very tenderly towards her when gradually she comprehends her predicament. The moving passage that describes her silent watching of Giles, the prince of Autumn, is illuminating here. The apprehensions are exact, but the driving force is nostalgic, the backward look across time and space from the point of exile, when 'Home over there', can no more be brought into adequate relation with 'Out here'.

> Her heart rose from its late sadness like a released bough; her senses revelled in the sudden lapse back to Nature

unadorned. The consciousness of having to be genteel because of her husband's profession, the veneer of artificiality which she had acquired at the fashionable schools, were thrown off, and she became the crude country girl of her latent early instincts.

Nature was bountiful, she thought. No sooner had she been cast aside by Edred Fitzpiers than another being, impersonating chivalrous and undiluted manliness, had arisen out of the earth ready to her hand.

You cannot feel that the writer here stands sufficiently at a distance from the experience his art deals with; but that does not diminish its importance for the novel as a whole. Grace, we are told, 'combined modern nerves with primitive feelings.' In some ways she stands near to her creator, and she is used, constantly, to sharpen our reponse to the novel's meaning. At several points in the story, she recalls earlier memories, and the passages serve to recapitulate the main themes and developments of the composition. Here, for instance, she remembers Giles.

He rose upon her memory as the fruit-god and the wood-god in alternation: sometimes leafy and smeared with green lichen, as she had seen him amongst the sappy boughs of the plantations: sometimes cider-stained and starred with apple-pips, as she had met him on his return from cider-making in Blackmore Vale, with his vats and presses beside him. . . .

From being but a frail phantom of her former self, she returned in bounds to a condition of passable hopefulness. She bloomed again in the face. . . . She thought of that time when he had been standing under his apple-tree on her return from school, and of the tender opportunity then missed through her fastidiousness. Her heart rose in her throat. She abjured all fastidiousness now. Nor did she forget the last occasion on which she had beheld him in that town, making cider in the courtyard of the Earl of Wessex Hotel, while she was figuring as a fine lady on the balcony above.

Mr. Melbury appears a more subtly observed character than his forerunner, Mrs. Yeobright. Hardy grasps so well the strong country passion for 'betterment', and its bitter outcome. The blindness of Melbury's ambition finds expression in his personal tragedy: the obligation towards Giles's father, the betrayal of trust, and the recognition of irreparable error. Indeed, the more closely one inspects *The Woodlanders*, the more admirable appears its structure both in the subtle blending of the tale with its woodland soil, and in the metaphorical detail of the tale itself. A vivid instance of that blindness is Melbury's trust in the new divorce law, in rescue, so to speak, from outside the village walls; and the sorry frustration of that trust. The outer world is constantly like that: fair in promise, but bitterly deceptive. Coming upon such a passage as this one, we remember Mrs. Hardy's note: 'If he could have had his life over again, he would prefer to be a small architect in a country town, like Mr. Hicks at Dorchester, to whom he was articled.'

'I wish you had never, never thought of educating me. I wish I worked in the woods like Marty South! I hate genteel life, and I want to be no better than she!'

'Why?' said her amazed father.

'Because cultivation has only brought me inconveniences and troubles. I say again, I wish you had never sent me to those fashionable schools you set your mind on. It all arose out of that, father. If I had stayed at home I should have married—'

She closed up her mouth suddenly and was silent; and he saw that she was not far from crying.

Melbury was much grieved. 'What, and would you like to have grown up as we be here in Hintock—knowing no more, and with no more chance of seeing good life than we have here?'

It isn't a subtle irony. Yet these effects of Hardy's achieve a simple but considerable poignancy, like his strong, dramatic conceptions. He saw the blindness of the Melburys as instrumental in the collapse of the agricultural societies; he found the 'more perfect insight into the conditions of existence' which education brought to bear, to be stunting to life; and the transience of those societies, with their valid, if limited 'good life', a transience intimated in dramatic forms throughout his best fiction, is his essential theme.

The counterpart to Melbury, fumbling in the great world without, is Mrs. Charmond fumbling in the village world, or lost in Hintock Woods, helpless and terrified. Her meeting there with Grace is one of Hardy's most imaginative contrivances. Grace is heavily committed in Mrs. Charmond's world, and she too loses herself in those woods. But though she is tired and frightened too, she knows these woods, they are her home. It is she who leads the stranger out, and her resource and poise offset Mrs. Charmond's bewilderment.

TESS OF THE D'URBERVILLES (1888–91)

HARDY's earlier *Novels of Character and Environment* deal ostensibly with past times. *The Woodlanders* and *Tess of the D'Urbervilles* have for their setting the years of the contemporary agricultural tragedy. In these, and particularly in the second, the artistic purity is sullied. The weaving of a ballad tale into the agricultural environment, together with the expression of Hardy's profound and vigorous feeling for the status of man in the natural order, no longer absorbs sufficiently the novelist's anxiety, his apprehension of collapse. Assertion tends to replace dramatic invention. In *Jude the Obscure* his characteristic narrative method is to be virtually transformed. There, Hardy enters the lists alongside George Eliot and Henry James with a tragic psychological fiction.

He responds in his own way to the tensions of his time, fortified by the example of a group of now-forgotten 'problem novelists' and deeply impressed by the work of Ibsen. The desire to develop his art in this way sprang from his seriousness and his compassion. But the endeavour in fact places that art in dependence upon its weaker resources. *Jude the Obscure* has deflected attention away from Hardy's most distinguished and personal contribution to the English novel, and towards a small part of his achievement that it is easier to connect with the familiar elements in our great fiction. That part, however serious, is less distinguished, and it cannot stand comparison with the achievements of his greatest contemporaries.

It is true to say that *Tess* is a flawed performance, but it is little to the purpose. The novel survives its faults magnificently. The simplicity and force of its conception give to it a legendary quality. Here is not merely the tragedy of a heroic girl, but the tragedy of a proud community baffled and defeated by processes beyond its understanding or control. The resonance of the tale makes itself felt over and over again. The superb opening, the death of Prince the horse, the lovely elegiac scene of the harvesting, the sequence in the dairy farm, the scene of the sleepwalking, the episodes of agricultural life at Flintcomb Ash, even the climax at Stonehenge, are powerful and original imaginative inventions. The rather tawdry theatricality of that climax, the deceptive offer of tragic symbolism, reveal themselves only on reflection. We scarcely try to understand—we feel that Hardy himself did not altogether measure this defeat, this calamity. But the insistent tenderness exacts concurrence, by a force like make-believe. The falsities, the intrusive commentaries, the sophisticated mannerisms in the prose, do only local damage.

Hardy composed nothing finer than the opening of *Tess*, and the style of it is entirely his own. The whole invention is at once substantial with social and historical perceptions, and quick with metaphorical life. The May Dance communicates a country mirth sustained by customary traditions and recognition of the seasonal rhythm. The three ominous visitors, one of them later to become an agent of destruction, suggest how the dance of vitality is jeopardized by the thrust of sophisticated urban life. Then the appearance of the spurious country squire adds to the sense of jeopardy. The masquerader, the economic intruder, the representative of processes at work destroying the bases of agricultural security, stands with the spiritual intruder. Alongside this image, there unfolds that of the old father's discovery of his ancient but unavailing ancestry: a disclosure of the community's past which helps to define what Tess represents in the ensuing tale, at the same time as it sharpens the intrusive and invading quality invested in Alec d'Urberville. We feel the lost independence and the helplessness of agricultural man in this decrepit figure, as also in old South, Durbeyfield's equivalent in the previous novel. The art ordering the whole is marvellously secure of its purpose. The metaphorical terms reside so naturally within the ballad narrative. The preparation for such later scenes as Tess harvesting at Marlott, Tess in the early dawn at Talbothays, is perfect. For Tess is not only the pure woman, the ballad heroine, the country girl: she is the agricultural community in its moment of ruin. For two years preceding the writing of *Tess*, Mrs. F. E. Hardy has recorded, 'Hardy explored in greater detail than ever before the scenes of the story, and was powerfully impressed by the massing evidence of the decay in agricultural life.' Here is the impulse behind the legend. It dramatizes the defeat of Tess, the country girl and repre-

sentative of an ancient country line, and her ruin by the
economic and spiritual invaders of country life.[1] It takes
its origin in a past lively with traditional activity; it ends
in Stonehenge, in passivity, the primitive place confirm-
ing a sense of doom which has gathered intensity all along.
What has happened in the agricultural society is by now
irrevocable. It is 1890, in south-west England.

The powerful, if faulty, sleepwalking scene records the
passivity and the doom most poignantly. It balances precariously between sentimentality and tragedy, yet its
impact transcends its place in the story. Hardy has
constructed a perfect imaginative equivalent for the
deepest perceptions which inform the novel as a whole.
Old John South's paralysis and death had something of
this fascinating quality, but here the enacted image
proves more distressing. For the most part the narrative
issues as if from the consciousness of Tess herself, impotent in the hold and motion of an alien force. She is
awake and strong-willed, yet passive, stunned. Her passivity (she makes no effort to alter the course of events)
appears to be one facet of her resilience. She is
the agricultural predicament in metaphor, engaging
Hardy's deepest impulses of sympathy and allegiance.
Clare is helpless too: a blind, unknowing force, carrying
the country girl to burial. Hardy's sense of curt, impersonal powers (such as preside in the world of balladry)
who order human destiny, here becomes a strength to
his fiction. Clare, so the narrative implies, is the impassive instrument of some will, some purpose, stemming
from the disastrous life of the cities, from the intellectual
and spiritual awareness—and confusion—of the world outside the agricultural community, and rather doomed to
destroy, than intending to destroy, the dignity and
vitality of country life. The invention, here, goes
beyond nostalgia. But the image is painful; all the

---

[1] d'Urberville's farm is as bogus as his villa is ostentatiously civic and
unrelated to the countryside.

suffering with which Hardy felt the defeat of agricultural life by nullifying urban forces, has gone into it, and the private despair that was the novelist's own inheritance from his sojourn 'outside'.

The movement of this novel, in which the tale develops against a shifting background instead of growing from one tract of countryside, also came of those desolate journeyings over the Wessex countryside. The pattern is deliberate. The unspoiled childhood and the May festivities belong to the village of Marlott. Tess's first restoration has for setting the dairy farms of the 'lush Froom Valley'. Her second restoration, when she builds a stoicism out of despair, occurs among 'the sterile expanses of Flintcomb Ash farmlands.' The catastrophe is in Budmouth with its 'fashionable promenades.'

When Tess first returns to agricultural activity after her seduction, in the harvesting at Marlott, the scenes are sufficiently impressive; the passage of her withdrawal from the field to feed her child is inspired. Yet it is spoiled by a commentary almost vulgar, as are the scenes describing the baptism and death of the child. Book Three, *The Rally*, however, sustains its power more steadily, a revelation of Hardy's sensuous understanding, that quality of feeling and instinct with which Lawrence thought Hardy to have been more generously endowed than any other English novelist. Talbothays is no paradisaical dairy farm. Language eager with details of activity, and native to its stated objects, language frank and vivid in sensuous perception, balances Tess's despair. Against the background of farm and dairyhouse, labour in the compact community, and the presence and voices of the workfolk, emerges the story of the fine young lord and the milkmaid and the three forlorn girls whose love is unrequited. To sketch it out like that is to suggest the proper way to take the 'story' element in Hardy's art.

The second movement whose power and beauty are sustained at length, balances the account of life at Crick's dairy farm. It records the life of Flintcomb Ash. The starting point is a matter of agricultural economics.

> Of the three classes of village, the village cared for by its lord, the village cared for by itself, and the village uncared for either by its lord or itself (in other words, the village of a resident squire's tenantry, the village of free or copy-holders, and the absentee-owner's village, farmed with the land) this place, Flintcomb Ash, was the third.

Flintcomb Ash directly reflects the new farming, contrasting in every essential with Talbothays. It is as essential to the meaning of the novel as the historical analysis of the opening, or the violent uprooting of the family driven out of the agricultural community at the end. And it affords an apt environment for this bitter part of the narrative. Tess's second recovery is painfully gradual, described in grave and laboured prose. The end of the movement is very moving; it brings us close to Hardy's distinction as a tragic writer. His incipient nostalgia is controlled by a scrutiny of the natural environment and the daily toil of the agricultural 'home', a scrutiny almost fierce in its anxiety. There is deep distress in this contemplation of Tess and the girls and the little labouring society of which they are a part. There is the nagging rigour of this life, and there is the will to endure and to persist and to labour on regardlessly, and the prose vividly reflects both.

An epilogue to this movement of the second recovery balances the harvest scene at Marlott which was prologue to the first. Harvest tide has returned. But now the human threshers stand side by side with the invading threshing machine. The narrative quality suggests the sleepwalking scene again. The sleepwalker, impersonal agent of destruction, is now the machine.

The sleepwalking scene gave a first impression of some mechanical force not to be baulked, once released. Now the impression grows clearer. The helpless Tess of the earlier scene is here the trapped, exhausted Tess whose task is to feed the machine. Her predicament gets a richer imagery from the group of labourers of 'an older day' who cannot resist, or accept, the new power, and who are bewildered and defeated. But in this second passage a bitter resentment makes the episode more disquieting. Consider the engineer, for instance.

> What he looked, he felt. He was in the agricultural world, but not of it. He served fire and smoke; these denizens of the fields served vegetation, weather, frost, and sun. He travelled with his engine from farm to farm, from county to county, for as yet the steam threshing-machine was itinerant in this part of Wessex. He spoke in a strange northern accent; his thoughts being turned inwards upon himself, his eye on his iron charge, hardly perceiving the scenes around him, and caring for them not at all. . . . The long strap which ran from the driving-wheel of his engine to the red thresher under the rick was the sole tie-line between agriculture and him.

The description which follows is quieter in its manner, but the use of detail of colour and gesture is more pointed. Hardy sounds a wistful note that suggests a personal disquiet.

> The old men on the rising straw-rick talked of the past days when they had been accustomed to thresh with flails on the oaken barn-floor; when everything, even to winnowing, was effected by hand labour. . . .

Then he emphasizes the less human quality of the life that has replaced that older life, an older life embodied earlier at Talbothays. Tess is again powerless and passive, caught by the machine's noise and motion, unable to speak, unable to rest.

Into this situation, reinforcing an aspect of its meaning, comes the invader, the son of the merchant from the North, 'dressed in a tweed suit of fashionable pattern, and twirling a gay walking cane.' Tess in Clare's arms as he sleepwalks, Tess in the clutch of the threshing machine, Tess before Alec d'Urberville—her predicament is the same. Detail by detail Hardy restores the environment to mind.

> Then the threshing-machine started afresh; and amid the renewed rustle of the straw Tess resumed her position by the buzzing drum as one in a dream, untying sheaf after sheaf in endless succession.

The marvellous passages that follow have a sensuous force and a depth of feeling Hardy rarely equalled.

> From the west a wrathful shine . . . had burst forth after the cloudy day, flooding the tired and sticky faces of the threshers, and dyeing them with a coppery light. . . . A panting ache ran through the rick. The man who fed was weary, and Tess could see that the red nape of his neck was encrusted with dirt and husks.

Wrathful takes its force from the mood of the contemplation. The *tired and sticky faces* seen as the shine breaks out suggest the weakening before the machine, and the *dyeing* of those faces reinforces that: they slip out of human expressions. *Coppery* both defines the observed tint, and reflects from the machine, holding the machine there beside their faces.

> She still stood at her post, her flushed and perspiring face coated with the corn-dust, and her white bonnet embrowned by it. She was the only woman whose place was upon the machine so as to be shaken bodily by its spinning, and the decrease of the stack now separated her from Marian and Izz. . . . The incessant quivering, in which every fibre of her frame participated, had thrown her into a stupefied reverie,

in which her arms worked on independently of her consciousness. She hardly knew where she was, and did not hear Izz Huett tell her from below that her hair was tumbling down.

By degrees the freshest among them began to grow cadaverous and saucer-eyed. Whenever Tess lifted her head she beheld always the great upgrown straw-stack, with the men in shirt-sleeves upon it, against the gray north sky. . . .

. . . And as the evening light in the direction of the Giant's Hill by Abbot's-Cernel dissolved away, the white-faced moon of the season arose from the horizon that lay towards Middleton Abbey and Shottsford. . . . But Tess still kept going. . . .

. . . She shook her head and toiled on.

The dramatic force with which Hardy's painful insights here find sensuous expression, is of no ordinary kind. The manner is one of simple and truthful tenderness; there is a fine adjustment between what the creating mind intends, and what the senses perceive. The truth carries over into the conversation afterwards, and to this:

The cold moon looked aslant upon Tess's fagged face between the twigs of the garden-hedge as she paused. . . .

Hardy sets the culminating family tragedy against the ominous background of the Lady Day migration of so many village folk. The erasure of long local life by these contemporary migrations, Hardy perceived, was a grave social and spiritual loss. It is no accident of art that the story of Tess should end amid scenes of uprooting. The narrative of the Durbeyfields' own moving from home is full of disquiet. The migration of so many others, the dissolving social order, is not particularly dwelt upon; but the ironical reception of the forlorn family at Kingsbere, its ancient home, dramatizes a personal bitterness of spirit. Only a place in the family vault, a home there, remains to the derelict inheritors. It is this homeless despair of a family which has lost its rights and independence in the village community, that gives Tess finally into the invader's power.

The sensation of moving unresistingly through a dream recurs in the passages that describe Tess impelled towards her doom and trapped for the last time. The hints of madness are indecisive enough to leave a nightmare quality around her experiences. The situation is blurred for her; the forces that have defeated her are beyond her comprehension.

JUDE THE OBSCURE (1892–5)

Jude, substantially different though it is, completes the imaginative record of the earlier novels. They treat of local stability and protagonists with roots deep down in their communities. *Jude* starts where the dispossessions and social ambitions of *The Woodlanders*, and the forced migrations of *Tess*, lead to, and treats of unlocalised protagonists continually on the move. It is a novel of place-names, changes, journeys and homelessness. The earlier novels celebrate rural manners and values; they work through deep but simple natures to establish respect for human dignity rather than human complexity. Their fables neglect the family, and the breeding and rearing of children, as if from Hardy's inner powerlessness to envisage a future as warmly and generously as he envisages the past. *Jude* takes the gifted and ambitious villager into the civic world, a milieu of intellect, introspection and subtle self-consciousness. It works through natures far from simple, and its fable concerns itself (to painful effect) with responsible married life, and the breeding of children. Jude's own experience is the medium through which Hardy discloses his vision, and Jude's is a far more sophisticated and sensitive nature than he had attempted hitherto. Neither in the rendering of the private consciousness, nor of intimate relationship, nor yet in the handling of an intellectual milieu, is Hardy a master. He is, rather, an explorer, and a bold one, and deserves honour for it. Under the strain here imposed upon his artistic resources, a strong autobiographical pressure breaks through. His notebooks show that he was well aware how much of himself went into his hero; and few would doubt, now, that much of his wife went into the astonishingly vivid and disconcerting study of Sue.

Jude's early despair has particular significance:

> He pulled his straw hat over his face, and peered through the interstices of the plaiting at the white brightness, vaguely reflecting. Growing up brought responsibilities, he found. Events did not rhyme quite as he had thought. . . As you got older . . . you were seized with a sort of shuddering, he perceived. All around you there seemed to be something glaring, garish, rattling, and the noises and glares hit upon the little cell called your life, and shook it, and warped it.

The biographical origin appears in Mrs. Hardy's *Early Years*.

> By the time he was fifteen, he tells us, he remembers lying back in the sun and wishing he need not grow up. He wanted to stay just as he was in the same place with the same few friends. The infinite possibilities mature life held for suffering and failure appalled him, made him sink back into such security as he knew.

Observing the near-Lawrentian force in the imaginative re-working of that memory (consider the verbs and participles), we feel how defensively near to Jude is the author himself. And as the novel unfolds there is indeed nowhere beyond Jude, no frame outside him, that Hardy can command confidently enough to transform his disturbance and his protest into great tragic art. Jude's avowed experience of bewilderment, defeat and intellectual ferment is the essential experience to be felt behind the novel as a whole.

'There is something the world ought to be shown,' Hardy had noted while first turning over the idea of the novel. *Jude* is often painful; its penetration is rather the direct report of a man deeply and personally involved in situations, relationships, and intellectual tensions too bewildering and tormenting for him, than the creative analysis of a great novelist. Neverthless it represents the endeavour of a deeply serious human spirit to measure up to the highest responsibilities he could assume; it breaks new ground in imaginative fiction, alike in its candour and in its brooding hopelessness. In the result, not only is the portrait of Sue extraordinarily bold and sensitive; Arabella and Philotson also elicit a strength of understanding and appreciation from Hardy such as the earlier novels give little hint of. It is right, with *Jude*, to speak of a failure of total imaginative organization, and it is easy enough to point to places that are false, or ill-judged, or merely embittered. But the parts are greater than the whole. There are scenes between the two protagonists whose psychological veracity still may astonish, and there are longer and shorter passages of tenderness and of penetration that only a novel such as Hardy here conceived could find place for. Finally—to re-establish its connection with the preceding novels—the opening Book of *Jude* is Hardy's finest narrative of a countryman's struggle towards the civic milieu: something needed to complete the pattern of his work. And the grave, retrospective irony that pervades the opening owes its authority to the later memorable rendering of that milieu: bewildering, tantalizing, frustrating, disappointing, and in the end insupportable. It is a grim but necessary complement to the simpler, more affirmative novels.

THE UNIQUENESS OF HIS ART

I

WE shall be wise to accept Mr. Maugham's dis-
claimers, in the preface he wrote for *Cakes and
Ale*. Edward Driffield is not Thomas Hardy. But every
reader of that accomplished little novel is likely to come
away with a few fresh insights bearing upon Hardy. 'He
was for long thought to write very bad English, and
indeed he gave you the impression of writing with the
stub of a blunt pencil.' What a penetrating comment it
appears to be! And it is time to draw some conclusions
about the style and bearing of Hardy's novels, whether of
phrase and paragraph, or of the manner and rhythm of the
whole book. In what ways does the presence of the
countryman beneath the skin of the writing, declare
itself?

I shall consider briefly three of these ways: first, the
handling of words and phrases and movement, second,
the treatment of country voices and the idiom of local
speech, and third, the larger rhythm of the ballad-tale.
Particularly I hope to define the presence of the countryman behind the way of the novel as a whole, and this in
spite of the conditions of serial publication, the apparent
manner, and the reading public Hardy had in view.

A quotation from *The Mayor of Casterbridge* provides the
happiest starting point for the first.

> The yeomen, farmers, dairymen, and townsfolk, who
> came to transact business in these ancient streets, spoke in
> other ways than by articulation. Not to hear the words of
> your interlocutor in metropolitan centres is to know

nothing of his meaning. Here the face, the arms, the hat, the stick, the body throughout, spoke equally with the tongue. To express satisfaction the Casterbridge market-man added to his utterance a broadening of the cheeks, a crevicing of the eyes, a throwing back of the shoulders, which was intelligible from the other end of the street. If he wondered . . . you knew it from perceiving the inside of his crimson mouth, and a target-like circling of his eyes. Deliberation caused sundry attacks on the moss of adjoining walls with the end of his stick, a change of his hat from the horizontal to the less so; a sense of tediousness announced itself in a lowering of the person by spreading the knees to a lozenge-shaped aperture and contorting the arms.

It is like a description of Hardy's own manner—indeed, it happens while he writes. The joviality is over-emphatic in just the way described. The clumsy inversions, the deliberate participles, strike attention like hefty physical movements, ponderous like that lowering of the knees. A versatility of gesture behind the words moves beneath the surface of the writing, this 'broadening of the cheeks, crevicing of the eyes, throwing back of the shoulders.' Here is the source of that astonishing weight in the finer passages, so hard to define: a baffling quality which leaves the reader in possession of deep impressions for which analysis cannot altogether account.

Abercrombie has a singularly illuminating passage in his monograph on Hardy. He is writing of the Wessex labourers.

It is evidently so laborious for them to express themselves at all. Their lives seem to go inwardly in a way in which words are of slight use to them. And when it comes to giving thought some outward shape of words, *they endeavour to contrive this by a sort of general attack upon language*; they hope that a great many inappropriate phrases will somehow suggest the appropriate thought. . . . Their thoughts are not like the urban, too poor to supply language with its material; they are too full of an undisturbed wealth that they do not know how to handle.

It might almost be an analysis of Hardy's own characteristic manner, so apposite it seems. And Hardy himself is aware of this incapacity of the countryman to command the language he needs. Oak, for instance, is silent when Bathsheba has rescued him.

> He would as soon have thought of carrying an odour in a net as of attempting to convey the intangibilities of his feeling in the coarse meshes of language.

'I can't match you, I know,' the same character says later, 'in mapping out my mind upon my tongue.' Just so, Hardy is conscious of unease with the language he uses. He studied *The Times*, Addison, and Scott, for a period, to improve his powers.

Hardy is not, in fact, a great imaginative writer in the natural sense. His power to order speech does not burgeon with his capacity to order his deepest experiences. Yet one wants to affirm, in justice to one's response to the cumulative as well as to the local effect of Hardy's fiction, that there is something beneath the surface, something of this rare ordering of experience. What may be declared with confidence—to resume Mr. Maugham's metaphor—about the pressure upon the blunt point of the pencil?

We must point to the sudden, transitory, almost accidental phrase or sentence where Hardy's command of a particular world and ordering of certain experiences comes to the surface and sinks again.

> The stillness was disturbed only by some small bird that was being killed by an owl in a neighbouring wood, whose cry passed into the silence without mingling with it.

These are apprehensions so recollected and valued that even an alien tongue can be made to express them; and in

them you discern the pressure that is all the while at
work.

> . . . His lips touching cheeks that were damp and smoothly
> chill as the skins of the mushrooms in the fields around.

Now this is a pressure that has to do with the expressiveness of literature, even though it is difficult to identify.
So with the wider range of the writing, and its 'general
attacks upon language'. The striving for impressiveness
may really have an origin in deep impressions. The
displays of erudition, the seeming incapacity for plain
speech, may not only aim to convince an urban reading
public that the author is one of them; it may also be that
the pressure at work takes the form of a determination
to forge a way of saying the thing that is not the casual,
the expected, way.

In those passages where we most readily detect the
imaginative writer, unhesitant and untrammelled, we
find usually a dialect use of language, or a use suddenly
very direct and simple. The conditions of primary pro-
duction, and local events and activities and ways of
thought, are immediately behind it. The prose may
render qualities very shrewdly: as when the atmosphere

> rubbed people's cheeks like damp flannel when they walked
> about.

His terms (as Mr. Blunden has said) 'disturb, bite in.'
Those are the moments of success. There are passages,
too, in which the pressure seems to move very near to
the surface of the writing, without quite disturbing
it—without achieving the memorable phrase. Such passages corroborate one's impression of a connection
between the transitory effect and the continuing pressure
beneath the surface. An example is the moment of stillness about Grace, in *The Woodlanders*, as Fitzpiers goes
away, leaving her alone by the body of Giles.

No sign of any other comer greeted her ear, the only perceptible sounds being the tiny cracklings of the dead leaves
which, like a feather-bed, had not yet done rising to their
normal level where indented by the pressure of her husband's
receding footsteps.

This is illuminating as a slow-motion film might be. It
isn't the real thing, it hasn't the convincing movement.
But it is a specially-heard stillness, and it is a woodland
stillness. And the slightly distorting weight · of the
invention allows the actual particulars to assert themselves the more clearly. The phrasing has a sort of heavy
stealth.

One longer passage illuminates the connection more
vividly. Again Hardy is occupied with sounds; twice
the pressure towards imaginative articulation moves near
the surface, and subsides,· and the third time it achieves
its effect precisely. The sound of the dead, dried heath-
bells is heard on the heath, in *The Return of the Native*.

A dwindled voice strove hard at a husky tune, which was
the peculiar local sound alluded to.

That is the first attempt, and (in its context) the metaphor has a considerable power; you can hardly mistake
the perception. But Hardy feels driven to search out
a more adequate expression. Sharpening his references
(the *dwindled voice* becomes *the throat of fourscore and ten*)
he writes again,

That note bore a great resemblance to the ruins of human
song which remain to the throat of fourscore and ten.

But a facet of the perception has slipped away—the
dwindling, the striving. *Ruins of human song* supplies,
instead, the faltering accent of some grander style. The
perception and the language it needs elude one another,
but the pressure will not let Hardy go. A moment, and—

> It was a worn whisper, dry and papery, and it brushed so distinctly across the ear. . . .

It is marvellously said. *Worn* unobtrusively modulates between the sound and the touch, between *whisper* and *dry and papery*. The tiny muscle of *distinctly* rejoins the audible and the tangible, taking us from *brushed* to *ear*. The delicate, tactile feeling of the whole phrase grows from the incipient metaphor (dust lurking in it) of *worn . . . papery . . . brushed* with its suggestion of sweeping shavings, torn scraps of paper, imperceptible odds and ends, over the floor with a soft brush. But Hardy, the pressure slowly subsiding, is intent upon explanation.

> . . . that, by the accustomed, the material minutiae in which it originated could be realized as by a touch.

By now, we cannot lightly pass over the ponderous gloss. We know that under the surface, under the *material minutiae* of this later phrase, a pressure is still active. But the language slips away, and on the surface the perceptions become disordered.

In the quality of Hardy's language, then, we meet the man whom Mr. Maugham remembered meeting.

> When the ladies retired to the drawing-room I found myself sitting next to Thomas Hardy. I remember a little man with an earthy face. In his evening clothes, with his boiled shirt and high collar, he had still a strange look of the soil.

We meet a countryman whose consciousness and voice and manner are meshed in the townsman's language. Hence the journalese, the literary airs, the stilted quality of phrase, the ponderous learning, the periphrasis, the virtual inability to make a plain statement. Yet, absorbed into the uncouthness is the very thing it seems to give the lie to: an accurate, affectionate honesty.

The special function of the voices of country folk in Hardy's imaginative art now suggests itself. The utterances of these men and women, especially the labourers, stand towards the longer rhythm of the novels as the local momentary phrase, so startlingly articulate, stands towards the page and the paragraph. These voices do something to vouch for the longer rhythm; and they tell us that Hardy's vitality finds nourishment within the agricultural society where they are heard. Consider, for a moment, even in his best novels, the speech of the urban characters. Evidently his use of rural voices cannot be reportage; if it were a matter of listening carefully and reproducing accurately, we should be at a loss to account for the failure to make an urban voice sound natural or convincing. He had quite as much opportunity to listen to and to record the voices of the town, but his version is artificial and often quite unlike human speech. He had not the reporter's ear at all. Rather, the country voice engaged his keener apprehensions. He felt deeply for what that voice represented, and he constructed an accent and a movement to record his feelings. He listened for and made dramatic a way of life behind the voice: no reader can long remain unaware of it. Often the art is naïve and direct.

'Thirty-one last tatie-digging, Mister Fairway.'

'Her mind can no more be heaved from that one place where it do bide, than a stooded waggon from the hole he's in. Lord love 'ee, neither court-paying, nor preaching, nor the seven thunders themselves, can wean a woman when 'twould be better for her that she should be weaned.'

These voices do not only address the ear with more or less naturalness. The conditions of life are there, in phrase and movement: local legend, belief and ritual, the history of the countryside and its changes, methods

of agriculture, of tenure, of commerce. Cumbersome
delivery is oddly allied to verve of phrase. It is the speech
of men who 'deal with their minds as with the soil for
harvest,' shrewd, laborious.[1] But it is a constructed
style of speech, unmistakably. Hardy is out to indicate
its significance imaginatively, not merely to suggest it
'from the life' for effects of local colour: witness his
very spare use of local words and his careful disposition
of phrase.

> 'And the best wine that berries could rise to; and the
> briskest Horner-and-Cleeves cider ever wrung down, leaving
> out the spice and sperrits I put into it, while that egg-
> flip would ha' passed through muslin, so little criddled
> 'twere.'

The movement unites delicacy and verve. Again how
poignant is the dignity here, and independent of any
strength that dialect *vocabulary* might supply:

> Marty did not fully comprehend, and she answered,
> 'He belongs to neither of us now, and your beauty is no
> more powerful with him than my plainness. I have come to
> help you, ma'am. He never cared for me, and he cared
> much for you; but he cares for us both alike now.'

That barely perceptible irritation, vexing the dignity,
completes the distinction.

The voices give a special truth to the longer movement
of the novels. His characters convince by what they say
and do, not by what Hardy says about them, or by any
analysis of motive or personality. They are not continually present, enforcing a meaning dramatically, as one
reads. They impinge suddenly upon the consciousness,
speaking, or acting, in a transitory way; for the rest, the
reader must work his thoughts. Their voices have thus
a special importance. It is no coincidence that Hardy's

---

[1] See *Thomas Hardy: A Critical Study* (1912), by L. Abercrombie.

finest achievements in character drawing are his most assured successes in voice, like Henchard and Marty South.

Yet he seems often to have been distracted by self-consciousness even in presenting the voices of characters important to his art. He remembers his reading public, and endeavours appropriate modifications. There are other moments when he seems himself to sense how much depends upon the voices for the effect of the fiction. There is one in *Far from the Madding Crowd*, when in a moment full of tragedy Bathsheba seems to overhear her own voice, floating. She is not Hardy's most complex creation, but as a changing, developing person she is among the outstanding successes of his novels. The changes, from vain and buoyant girl, through country farmer and rejected wife and numbed woman to the courageous and loyal wraith of the last episodes, are made the more actual in her changing voice. *The Return of the Native* depends least of the finer novels upon the speaking voice; it depends, rather, upon the hammering into writing, narrative more than dramatic, descriptive and not oral, of deeply meditated situations. The staple of speech is absent. Yet among the most authentic passages is the account by Susan's boy of how Mrs. Yeobright died. The voice is casual and unemotional and passive; for a moment, it invests the death with remote dignity.

There is a leisurely movement from scene to scene in a novel like *Far from the Madding Crowd* that might with truth be called a country rhythm. At the same time, the conditions of serial publication have their bearing upon the structure of the novels. But there is something more underlying this rhythm, this structure, something with its origin more distinctly in the agricultural environment.

When Hardy concluded his praise of George Eliot, 'but she is not a born story-teller', what had he in mind?

Hardy's imagination was nurtured in a tradition of balladry. His art as a story-teller is a balladist's art, formal, social, rhetorical, working upon a stereotyped kind of narrative material. Although apparently subdued to the alien mode of conventional Victorian fiction, his invention is lively and effective only when it is freely released to develop the ballad techniques native to it. It is worth a reader's while to come to terms with this aspect of Hardy's art, for false expectations have misled many. Much of the poetry, and several short stories (like the famous *The Three Strangers* from *Wessex Tales*) reveal the balladist's presence obviously enough. There are some suggestive notes of his own.

> We tale-tellers are all Ancient Mariners, and none of us is warranted in stopping Wedding Guests unless he has something more unusual to relate than the ordinary experience of every average man or woman.

The Prefaces to the collections of short stories—indeed, the Prefaces generally—bear witness to the traditional origins of many of his tales. Much that may seem bewildering about the novels has its explanation in the balladry that underlies them. Hardy's attitude towards folk beliefs and customs, intimate and unforced and never incredulous, seems natural in this setting. Above all, the pervasive irony has its origin in balladry. This is not to deny that in the later novels Hardy handles irony with sophistication and bitterness for private and deliberate ends: he does, and not always successfully. But there is also the genuine irony of the ballads, a clear and serious irony familiar to the characters it pursues. One may speak of it as the irony of the legend recounted in the country inn. Hardy's tales depend upon old traditional memories, they lean towards the village inn and his father's art. That leaning will do more than German philosophy to explain why Fate so dominates the stories as protagonist.

One by one the striking things about Hardy's art as a story-teller fall naturally into place as functions of balladry. There is the reliance, especially at the outset, upon the sharp definition of scene and background. There is the easy alliance of the grotesque and disproportionate with the substantial and natural, and the unselfconscious boldness with which they are offered. There are the slighter rhythms and movements of the story suggesting that the sung stanza is never far behind. There are the neat, rounded, and intertwining groups of events, the simple and decisive balancing of characters. There is the vivid sense of the meaning of scenery, the human and the natural involving one another. There is the narrative method whereby encounter (whether of person with person, or person with Fate) is the life of the tale. The ballad situations and the ballad coincidences are carried off partly by boldness and verve; partly by an art which holds all spare attention concentrated upon the vividness of the presentation itself. This happens in the Stonehenge scene of *Tess*. But turn, for a more brilliant illustration, to that extraordinary scene in *The Return of the Native*—one of the most personal and memorable in all Hardy—the dicing by glow-worm light. Nobody but a countryman nurtured in the traditional arts of balladry could have invented it; and only an imaginative writer leaning back towards the conditions of life that once bred balladry and its audience could have composed the passage as Hardy has.

The fables and the persons of the novels bear the same impress. In this sense, too, the Wessex books are ballads writ large. Here is the maiden poised between the strong, quiet and devoted soldier and the rakish sailor.

Here is the seduced milkmaid and the three forlorn maidens bearing her company. Here is Troy, the handsome and dashing soldier in scarlet. Here is the ominous mantrap in the woods by night; and here are two fleeing lovers drowned in a weir amid storm and darkness. Here are the paralysed old John South and the sinister Furmity Woman. These are so evidently the figures and symbols of balladry, indeed, that the resemblance needs no labouring. The characterization itself has the same ancestry. Giles and Oak are the devoted lovers of ladies above their station; Marty South and Fanny Robin may be called their counterparts. The novelist's attitude to them is as the balladist's. He takes their goodness, their devotion, their extreme loyalty, for granted, as he takes Eustacia's passion or Bathsheba's waywardness (and these two women are equally ballad heroines). He takes their elementary qualities on trust in such a way as to make them surprisingly real, like their simplicity. His detached, confident attitude to the rural protagonists strengthens the fiction. Consider the account of Oak in the opening pages of *Far from the Madding Crowd*. It veers from stolid reverence to quiet derision in a paragraph. It is an attitude natural to a tale for the inn and its company; and it allows for little subtle development or alteration in the characters once the story has begun. The changes must be clear and manifest.

THE TRUMPET-MAJOR (1879)

It is worth pursuing this theme for a brief note about *The Trumpet-Major*, which has an ease of movement unlike anything in the other distinguished novels. It remains much closer to balladry throughout. You can even feel the succession of stanzas; and there is the parabola of its movement—a pattern later worked more powerfully,

but less naturally, in *The Mayor of Casterbridge*. There, the
tale begins and ends with the open road; and Henchard's
oath, his curse, and his will, divide its movement. Here,
the intruding colour and noise of the dragoons interrupts
the rural peace, to start the story; and peace is restored
at the end, as the regiment leaves and the sound of the
major's steps recedes. The tale has the air of an anecdote
developed for an evening's reminiscence at the inn; it is,
at the same time, an anthology of recollections. Hardy
assumes for the occasion a more ideal audience than he
usually allowed himself. He talks as to the manner born.
He does not force tragic issues. The undertone of war
gives the novel a certain depth, implies an area of darkness about the tale. The character-drawing seems finely
proportioned to the emotional weight of the fable. The
grave events of the world without are envisaged from
inside the village, but the sombre background is never
long forgotten. The descriptive preparation for the scene
of the King's Review serves well to indicate these
qualities. The places reflect memories, some near,
some remote; the recently erected beacons disturb the
landscape with a suggestion of tension, and suddenly alter
the perspective. A vivid feeling for the recollected past
runs through the whole description. Consider the interplay of history with the present moment, and the simple
but deep feeling, when the final meditation flowers out
of the narrative:

> The troops then cleared off the field, the spectators fol-
> lowed, and by one o'clock the downs were again bare.
> They still spread their grassy surface to the sun as on that
> beautiful morning not, historically speaking, so very long ago;
> but the King and his fifteen thousand armed men, the horses,
> the bands of music, the princesses, the cream-coloured
> teams—the gorgeous centre-piece, in fact, to which the
> downs were but the mere mount or margin—how entirely

have they all passed and gone!—lying scattered about the
world as military and other dust; some at Talavera, Albuera,
Salamanca, Vittoria, Toulouse, and Waterloo; some in
home churchyards; and a few small handfuls in royal
vaults.

The downs before, with their enduring quality, and the
battlefields and churchyards after, and the sincere feeling
of it, give resonance to this elegy. That note sounds
several times again; it distinguishes the novel. But, as is
consonant with the quiet and confident texture of the
story-telling, Hardy sounds the note in this tone of im-
partial, almost surprised, equanimity. The other, more
remarkable, novels have greater strengths; but they do
not sound quite this note again, they lack the equanimity.
This poise of the story-teller is fitful in them, while here
it governs the long rhythm of the whole, even to the last
paragraph. Then the serious, elegiac note sounds yet
more gravely, and the same quiet bearing checks a
deeper feeling.

> The candle held by his father shed its waving light upon
> John's face and uniform as with a farewell smile he turned
> on the doorstone, backed by the black night; and in another
> moment he had plunged into the darkness, the ring of his
> smart step dying away upon the bridge as he joined his
> companion-in-arms, and went off to blow his trumpet till
> silenced for ever upon one of the bloody battlefields of
> Spain.

The movement suggested by the punctuation defines the
quiet rapidity of voice, taut with unvoiced grief. The
light wanes into the black night, the sounds disappear
into a final silence, and the story-teller's perspective
removes to a fitting distance what has been seen and heard.

Hardy seems, then, more than usually absorbed and
delighted by the mere invention and relation of this tale.
His tone implies an audience that shares his main convic-

tions, and shares his energetic pleasure in the unfolding of events. The narrative art is zestful; it needs appreciating leisurely, detail by detail. The imagined audience may never have existed, but Hardy was prepared to assume it in a way he never could assume it when he was more purposefully and earnestly engaged. Hardy's seriousness of purpose was, of course, a fundamental strength to his fiction, but that need not deter us from a just appreciation of the lesser distinction of *The Trumpet-Major* and the best stories. Moreover, in quieter ways, Hardy's general seriousness does make itself felt here also. Throughout the novel you may detect that modest but unfailing sense of the transitory joys and pains of human life, and that dignified respect for men and women overshadowed by sadness, which are characteristically his own.

THE SHORT STORIES

THE best of Hardy's stories belong to the period of his maturity and fame as a novelist; a few are memorable and distinguished by-products of his art; their potent images connect them immediately with the later novels. Very many more sketch out themes and predicaments that illuminate or endorse the substance of Hardy's creative work. The more candidly anecdotal method makes for a grace and confidence like that of *The Trumpet-Major*; there is no call for extended developments of ballad material which has its own complete and intractable substance. Where, among the stories, the impulse of the prose balladist has freest play, we detect an inventive energy and delight. Consider *The Three Strangers* (1883) *The Distracted Preacher* (1879), *The Romantic Adventures of a Milkmaid* (1883), and *A Few Crusted Characters* (1891). But even the sketches last-named, buoyant and humorous anecdotes for the most part, are enclosed within an

elegiac framework and relate to the figure of the returned
native, dismayed by his experience of the outer world,
longing for the agricultural certainties and simplicities,
and much possessed by death and the passing of things.
The last pages have a singularly effective reticence.

The reader soon detects how surely even these slighter
successes revolve about Hardy's imaginative centre, how
close their qualities lie to his deepest interests. There is
the strong feeling for decay, the oddly morbid pre-
occupation. There is the anxious feeling for local ties
and traditions, bonds imaged with gay humour in the
illicit smuggling of *The Distracted Preacher*. There is the
dismay about 'rising in the world' and the constantly
returning intuition of the dangerous invader of rural
security: he has assumed demonic, though never deliberately hostile, powers in *The Romantic Adventures of a
Milkmaid*, the most truly ballad-like fiction in all Hardy.
And there is the profound and tender feeling for the
helplessness and frustration of the agricultural figures,
the bystanders. These stories have the ingredients, but
we enjoy them more for their energy, for their absorbing
narrative invention.

It is not altogether so with the more subtle and original
stories collected as *Life's Little Ironies*, nor with three other
tales of a similar inspiration, *Fellow Townsmen* (1880),
Interlopers at the Knap (1884), and *The Waiting Supper*
(1888). Here, in one sequence after another, we find
the channels of invention running direct and clear from
source: from the tensions and divisions between agricultural and city life, from the bitter implications of social
ambition among country folk. We find vivid figurations of
the mesmeric stranger from the alien world, and of the
impotent countryman. We find moving imagery of intrusion and invasion, of frustration and longing, of quiet persistence and quiet despair. The sombre genius of Crabbe

presides over the melancholy poise and irony of the
narrator; invention and treatment alike owe much to
him, especially the desolate, abrupt conclusions. *The
Waiting Supper* has a sharp power all its own. It is a
sort of miniature for *The Woodlanders*, then just completed, controlled by its image of the compulsive invader, the presence now acknowledged, now unseen,
which troubles agricultural cohesion and disrupts the
natural relation of the two protagonists. Not here,
however, nor in the Demon Lover of *The Romantic Adventures of a Milkmaid*, but in the brilliant *The Fiddler of the
Reels* (1893) does Hardy achieve his most spectacular
and disturbing treatment of this narrative imagery. Every
detail of the tale makes its metaphorical point; the initial
conception of the strangely gifted musician able to cast
chromatic magic over traditional village dance tunes, the
Pied Piper of the village dance, has striking possibilities.
The tale of the beguilement of the village girl by the
demonic fiddler from the alien world is grounded
securely in the traditional music and dance and the
social milieu of Stickleford life. Car'line Aspent, mes-
merized by the music and the personality of Mop Olla-
moor, and flawed by social ambition, abandons Ned Hipcroft, her village lover. He leaves Wessex for London,
and it is there, years later, that the betrayed Car'line
comes to him, bringing her child by the fiddler. She
comes by means of the new railroad connecting Wessex
with London, and in the year of the Great Exhibition.
When they visit the Exhibition together, she feels Mop
casting his menacing shadow over them again; and when
the three seek to return to Wessex and the home
simplicities, the fiddler reappears at the village inn, mes-
merizes the girl who dances to exhaustion while he plays,
and vanishes with the child, the symbol of their union,
but now also infinitely dear to Hipcroft too. The con-

I

clusion is frustration; behind them, and behind the tale, stand the railroad and the Exhibition, symbols (Hardy says) of 'a sudden bringing of ancient and modern into absolute contact', a contact that is the despair of the ancient.

This boldness of narrative imagery sets apart the finest of the tales. Sometimes, as in *The Fiddler of the Reels*, the image is pursued through to its heart, and disturbs with its impact. More often, it is released but not followed far. The recently published tale for boys, *Our Exploits at West Poley* (1883), is an example. The imaginative kernel is the exploration of the ancient cave interiors, with their long undisturbed insignia of the past, and their ancient control of agricultural potential in the villages; but the kernel remains, so to speak, unopened. The elegiac mood of the opening and close, the brief, frankly adult statement of Hardy's themes, indicate sufficiently what a disturbing tale might have been told. Even as it is, elegiac recollection is the substance of the tale. But once the events unfold, Hardy subdues his interests to those of the imagined boy-protagonist. The first few pages are the significant ones, touching in, as they do, the frustration of seeking to rise in the world, the tragedy of the countryman exiled from agriculture, through the sombre, shadowy figure of The Man who had Failed. This saddened returned native presides at a distance throughout, a potential interpreter never called upon, He might have unfurled the image, we feel; and through him, at its end, the tale points lightly but deliberately to the agricultural stoicism, 'quiet perseverance in clearly defined courses.'

In the striking tale called *The Son's Veto* (1891) the elegiac note sounds most beautifully. The events of a characteristic narrative of the marriage of a country girl to a man outside the rural sphere, slowly unfold into an image of a curiously haunting quality. The conclusion indicates the desolation of the loyal country lover who was rejected; but, underpinning his predicament, the poignant climax depicts the widowed girl alone in the town house, discovering that her former country lover journeys to and from Covent Garden with waggon-loads of vegetables. Filled with hopeless longing for her lost home and its simplicities, thwarted for ever by her son, she makes a secret journey with her loyal lover, seated among the cabbages, in the early hours of morning, to Covent Garden. The episode has Hardy's piercing notes of detail; on reflection, it seems to preside over the whole tale, a suggestive image.

The boldness of the narrative strokes and the economy of means distinguish Hardy's best stories and make them a definite enrichment of the novels, as well as an illuminating commentary upon their themes. He is unambitious and at ease, here, often oblivious of the magazine public and rarely troubled by its demands. He invents buoyantly, sensible of 'local hearts and heads', and sometimes strikes out a caustic, sardonic style unusual in his work.

For Hardy's weaknesses express a necessary over-reaching of his true competence. By the range and depth of his thinking and of his experience of life, he felt himself committed to a style of composition quite unlike that of a countryman relating a tale or recounting a ballad to countrymen. His strength of character, as well as his practical needs, led him to write as a citizen, within conventions shaped largely by the life and interests of cities. He could not altogether succeed. The sort of integrity that distinguishes great literature is not submissive to mere strength of character. Hardy's style evidences a continual uncertainty about the interests, the expectations, the likely response of his readers. The emphases and the falsities begin here, and the intrusion of clumsy facetiousness in some places where Hardy was least of all desiring to be patronizing. He had plenty of imaginative force, but very little tact. The conditions for tact were lacking: that is what makes his study of Defoe, Scott, Fielding, and *The Times*, and his struggle to produce a replica of 'style' as he found it in them, so useless. The style he thus sought to learn was a way of speech between writers and readers who shared fundamental convictions, who were at home together. Even could a style be learnt like that, such a style was not for Hardy. One may perhaps be pardoned the wish that he had studied Richard Jefferies instead.

That Hardy was deeply conscious, and resentfully so, of his situation as a writer, is my own feeling. Uncertain as it is, the surviving evidence suggests that his first, and for ever unpublished, novel, and its reception and refusal, may have influenced the remainder of his writing profoundly. It may have taught the author a lesson he never forgot, but never spoke of, until the reception of *Jude the Obscure* supplanted the memory. But this is to enter the realms of not very useful speculation.

In sum, there goes with the seriousness of Hardy's finest novels a thorough confusion of manner. The author is constantly aware of certain divisions between himself and his audience, and he fumbles away to conceal discrepancies. There is ever the look of the soil that Mr. Maugham noted: the exact, assured phrase, the idiom of labourers, the perspective of a balladry native to the Wessex societies. But the boiled shirt, the high collar, and the evening clothes, surround that look and muffle it. 'I remember a little man, with an earthy face', Mr. Maugham wrote; and when he had finished his sketch, he added, 'It struck me at the time, that there was in him a strange mixture of self-assurance and shyness'. That is the man, and that is the imaginative prose artist. There is an inflexibility of mind and character in Hardy's writing; his is an inflexible prose. But there is a great deal more than that.

II

I think it is a mistake to speak too freely of tragic grandeur as the mark of Hardy's novels, even at their finest. But neither can their quality be dismissed as a mere nostalgic poignancy. That their impulse is nostalgic, seems clear; but a peculiar strength grows alongside that impulse. That is the strength I want to illuminate now, and to do so I shall compare some moments in Hardy's art with some moments in Wordsworth's narrative poetry. Certain affinities in their situations as artists are striking enough. Both were born and bred in the country and left it during the impressionable years of early manhood. Both entered into civic life and insights, and came under the influence of leading contemporary thinkers. The earliest creative writing of both was critical of the urban social order; both eventually turned, frustrated, back to the country, and sought to embody in their writing the decisive value of that return. The finest art of both is riveted in the past and in memories and experiences of the past. Both responded to nature as the field of permanency, and carried over into their art a sense of escape, a sense sharpened by insights won in the world without. But their distinction is not to be found simply in their apprehension of nature, or of human life lived intimately in touch with nature. That apprehension provided a calming and restorative bearing for their different acknowledgements and explorations of the sombre element in human life. Each could, in his measure,

> afford to suffer
> With those that he saw suffer,

having found a means for tranquillity of spirit; though Hardy's leaning was towards uncontrollable distress, and Wordsworth's towards exhausted inertia.

The means for tranquillity, the resident strength, the restorative place in their art: it is this that I seek to distinguish. In Hardy's novels, it is an apprehension of activity, of agricultural skills, of social relations. The restorative place in Wordsworth's art, on the other hand, is an apprehension of transcendent presences in a countryside divested of activity and society. Only secondarily, even remotely (so far as the poetry takes us) does his art turn upon human life and actions within that scene. Though Wordsworth may present a Leech-Gatherer so that the figure disturbs our consciousness to an uncanny degree, the disturbance seems to depend upon inactivity: he gathers no leeches. But when Marty South comes upon the consciousness, she cuts spars; or Giles plants saplings; or Clym cuts furze.

> . . . A girl seated on a willow chair, and busily working by the light of the fire, which was ample and of wood. With a bill-hook in one hand, and a leather glove, much too large for her, on the other, she was making spars, such as are used by thatchers, with great rapidity. She wore a leather apron. . . . On her left hand lay a bundle of the straight, smooth hazel rods. . . . On her right, a heap of chips and ends . . . in front, a pile of the finished articles. . . . She took up each gad, looked critically at it from end to end, cut it to length, split it into four, and sharpened each of the quarters with dexterous blows. . . .
>
> The young woman laid down the bill-hook . . . and examined the palm of her right hand which. . . . was red and blistering.

That is the first impression *The Woodlanders* offers of Marty. Similarly Giles arranged to plant them with his own hands. He had a marvellous power of making trees grow. Although he would seem to shovel in the earth quite carelessly there was a sort of sympathy between himself and the fir, oak, or beech that he was operating on; so that the roots took hold of the soil in a few days.

These are Hardy's saliences. His shepherd is most compelling when thatching ricks, or branding lambs, or

at the bottom of her garden, grinding his shears for the sheep-shearing. . . . The scurr of whetting spread into the sky from all parts of the village. . . . Oak stood . . . his figure slightly bent, the weight of his body thrown over on the shears, and his head balanced sideways, with a critical compression of the lips and contraction of the eyelids to crown the attitude.

Wordsworth's point of focus is the stillness, the silence. His shepherd is most compelling in motionless loneliness, inert with grief. His Leech-Gatherer is a motionless stone. A moment's sight of a horse grazing concentrates an experience of unearthly suspense:

> . . . at his feet
> His shadow lay, and moved not.

The world of persons, in his verse, is a world of lone individuals—a Wanderer, a Blind Beggar, Margaret, Michael, a Solitary Reaper. His countryside has small social reality. Its figures lack human purpose; they have become vehicles for recollected apprehensions of Natural Presences—apprehensions that are sometimes coldly non-personal:

> . . . the silence and the calm
> Of mute insensate things.

There is a hint of insulation from human living. I am not depreciating Wordsworth's art. His most memorable passages grip and explore experiences of a transcendent

reality known through nature. Such experiences of
unplumbed depths provided a resource for the steady
contemplation of human vicissitudes, so that Wordsworth was able to expose his nerve to the drill of suffering, and to dramatize the exposure with a tranquilly
poised simplicity and restraint, yet with little offer of
alleviation.

The rhythm of Hardy's fiction has its pauses, its Wordsworthian places. But something quite distinct and different emerges from them. Recall, for a moment, the
stillest and loneliest of all his passages, where Marty
South stands solitary and motionless by the grave of Giles.
Here, if anywhere, we may expect a Wordsworthian
resonance.

> . . . A motionless figure, standing by the gate.
> 'I think it was Marty South,' said the hollow-turner
> parenthetically.
> 'I think 'twas; 'a was always a lonely maid,' said Upjohn.
> And they passed on homeward, and thought of the matter
> no more.

The loneliness itself, you find, is given a social setting,
and in the giving we are reminded of a certain hardness
ingrained in the countryman's fellow-feeling. That hardness carries a possibility of poise and restraint in face of
distress and pain.

> . . . But still no Grace. Yet her sense of comradeship
> would not allow her to go on to the grave alone, and still
> thinking the delay had been unavoidable, she stood there
> with her little basket of flowers in her clasped hands, and her
> feet chilled by the damp ground, till more than two hours
> had passed. . . . As this solitary and silent girl stood there in
> the moonlight, a straight slim figure, clothed in a plaitless
> gown, the contours of womanhood so undeveloped as to be
> scarcely perceptible, the marks of poverty and toil effaced by
> the misty hour . . . she looked almost like a being who had

rejected with indifference the attribute of sex for the loftier quality of abstract humanism.

Despite the passing voices, the comradeship invoked for the rite, and the emphasis upon the physical event, here at the culmination of his most characteristic novel Hardy seems to be moving to a distance from the human happening as Wordsworth might. *Effaced by the misty hour* controls the feeling; the marks of poverty and toil are lost. The moonlight hour of mist, the silent and solitary girl, come together to construct that hardly-identified shadow-graph figure who counts for so much in the expressiveness of Wordsworth's moments of great power.

Only then comes the stroke so illuminating for our present enquiry. A human gesture disturbs the fixity, and the mist and the motionlessness that have gone before redouble the effect of the movement. It is a gesture of habitual reverence, ageless. More, it is a gesture that takes to itself the whole weight of the novel. Readers of the passage know already what has become of Grace; her abandonment of the country is symbolized here. Her absence, while Marty does alone what they should have done together, sharpens our response. The unrequited fidelity of such as Giles and Marty, the relative falsity and failure of such as Grace, take tragic stature; they take it when, in turn, the gesture breaks the fixity, the words break the silence, and finally the activities of agricultural living issue from the words, and break down the moonlight, the solitude, the mistiness, the stillness.

> She stooped down, and cleared away the withered flowers that Grace and herself had laid there the previous week, and put her fresh ones in their place.

The simple phrases take on a metaphorical richness; then the spoken elegy, with the tone and movement of the voice heard in the country—heard, valued, reconstructed.

'Now my own, own love,' she whispered, 'you are mine and on'y mine; for she has forgot 'ee at last, although for her you died! But I—whenever I get up I'll think of 'ee, and whenever I lie down I'll think of 'ee. Whenever I plant the young larches I'll think that none can plant as you planted; and whenever I split a gad, and whenever I turn the cider wring, I'll say none could do it like you. If ever I forget your name, let me forget home and heaven! But no, no, my love, I never can forget 'ee; for you was a good man, and did good things!'

Consider the beginning. Hardy's insight is sensitive: he doesn't soften the possessiveness and self-concern deep down in even such selfless devotion as Marty's. With what aptness the release of her private grief is caught into the apostrophe—*own . . . own . . . Mine . . . mine*. Then the pang of jealousy and the tinge of relief are indicated in that second phrase, *for she has forgot 'ee at last, although for her you died*. Her voice is that of the country, claiming its own; but it has its personal grace and stress. The inflection is delicately sustained in the counter-movement, *But I—*, and gradually a new feeling gathers alongside Giles and all he represents. It is a feeling for Marty's own persistence in daily activity, in that numb carrying-on despite hopelessness, of which by the end of this novel we have some understanding. Marty's persistence accompanies Giles's presence. *Whenever I plant . . . and whenever I split a gad, and whenever I turn the cider wring. . . .* This is the point of strength, where the illusion of stillness, of the transfixed and transfigured shape in the misty moonlight, issues into activity. Giles represented this, and Marty will go on with this, day after day. The sensation of the ceaseless rhythm of agricultural labour in the community is the focus of the elegy.

Then the girl's last cry gives relief to the private elegiac emotion that informs the whole: 'If ever I forget your name let me forget home and heaven! But no, no, my love, I never can forget 'ee; for you was a good man and did good things!' *The Woodlanders* has given meaning to that goodness. The stillness is illusory, motion is real. *And did good things* is final, and that doing absorbs frustration and numbs the ache of hopelessness. We may remember that only a few pages before, in a fine passage of similar stillness, Fitzpiers had seen Marty, framed, as it were, in an open window by candlelight. And the girl was polishing the dead man's tools. The Giles whose memory she celebrates, whose spirit lives on in her, is known by his tools.

The still centre in Wordsworth's art is different.

> And afterwards, the wind and sleety rain,
> And all the business of the elements,
> The single sheep, and the one blasted tree,
> And the bleak music from that old stone wall. . . .

Passages like this—and there are several in Wordsworth's greatest verse—render with bare power an experience like that informing the end of *The Book of Job*. The natural order exists in its own right, in being continually, alien, regardless of the human condition and acknowledging no human suffrage.

> By what way is the light parted
> Or the east wind scattered upon the earth?
> Who hath cleft a channel for the waterflood
> Or a way for the lightning of the thunder?
> Or caused it to rain on a land where no man is,
> On a wilderness where there is no man?
> To satisfy the waste and desolate ground
> And to cause the tender grass to spring forth?

This vast natural world requires no private sanction. So, too, with Wordsworth. The immeasurable height of woods decaying, never to be decayed, the rocks and stones and trees, are imperiously real on their own account, do not defer to human experience.

Now Hardy, the author of *The Return of the Native*, clearly shares in a measure this profound feeling. We have had more than one reading of his novels in which this sense of men and women as tiny figures in a tremendous, casual world that cares nothing for their struggles, is made to appear his main theme. D. H. Lawrence's remarkable study, reprinted in *Phoenix*, puts the view most forcibly. Here he writes of *The Return of the Native*.

What is the real stuff of tragedy in the book? It is the Heath. . . . The Heath persists. Its body is strong and fecund, it will bear many crops beside this. Here is the sombre, latent power that will go on producing, no matter what happens to the product. Here is the deep, black source from whence all these little contents of lives are drawn. And the contents of the small lives are spilled and wasted. There is savage satisfaction in it: for so much more remains to come, such a black, powerful fecundity is working there that what does it matter?

Upon the vast, incomprehensible pattern of some primal morality greater than ever the human mind can grasp, is drawn the little, pathetic pattern of man's moral life and struggle, pathetic, almost ridiculous. The little fold of law and order, the little walled city within which man has to defend himself from the waste enormity of nature, becomes always too small. . . . The vast, unexplored morality of life itself, what we call the immorality of nature, surrounds us in its eternal incomprehensibility, and in its midst goes on the little human morality play, with its queer frame of morality and its mechanized movement; seriously, portentously, till some one of the protagonists chances to look out of the charmed circle, weary of the stage, to look into the wilderness raging round. Then he is lost. . . . And this is the quality Hardy shares with the great writers, Shakespeare or Sophocles or Tolstoi, this setting behind the small action of his protagonists the terrific action of unfathomed nature;

setting a smaller system of morality, the one grasped and formulated by the human consciousness, within the vast, uncomprehended and incomprehensible morality of nature or of life itself. . . .

One may hold that this brilliant meditation, though developing insights springing from the novels, is conducted at some distance from the novels themselves. One may attach more significance than Lawrence does to the fecundity of this natural order; one may usefully identify the smaller morality, the little walled city, with the enclosed agricultural communities and their traditional faith and ethics. Yet when all is said and done, this reading is faithful to the resonance of Hardy's fiction, the resonance which gives a vague but perceptible depth to its situations.

But human faithfulness to that smaller morality, 'that curious mechanical regularity of country people in the face of hopelessness,' is more the stuff of his art than is the vast wilderness. When Oak watches the skies, at night, solitary, his world is described with a variety of little sensuous touches that bring before us the stir and bustle of human living and doing. When he perceives the stars, it is with the measured regard of a shepherd whose vocation involves a practical dependence upon them. He spends one moment appreciating the silence, the loneliness, the absence of 'the sights and sounds of men', the next he is restoring an ailing calf in a shed whose light had seemed to be that of one among the myriad stars. He is not like Wordsworth's shepherd, whose vocational crafts serve to bring out his paralysed dereliction at the end of the tale; Michael, who

> had been alone
> Amid the heart of many thousand mists
> That came to him and left him on the heights.

That strong sensation of natural goings-on regardless of
human life made possible the poetry of the petrified
grief at the end of *Michael*, and the nearly inert restraint
of its narration. Human stature is there reduced to a sort
of animal helplessness, so sharp is the suffering envisaged.
There is never quite that reduction in Hardy. Wordsworth confronts the dazed animal that is all that is left
of the shepherd of unusual strength and industry, with
little evidence of grief, and quite without the thin vein
of gratuitous cruelty that Hardy sometimes opens, per-
mitting the impulses of the sacrificing priest. The events
seem to engrave themselves into an inanimate order:

> . . . many and many a time he thither went,
> And never lifted up a single stone.

He is a motionless figure, yet of unusual strength. One remembers the unusual strength at this point in the poem,
and the details of the shepherd's vocation; they accentuate the stillness. Compared with Hardy, Wordsworth
presents the more absolute desolation, and presents it
with more reserve, and that not just because the medium
of verse acts by concentration. The poetry at the end persists with the faintness and exhaustion of pain, its pulse
'delicate, almost ceasing to beat, maintained only by
the flutter of tenuous hopes and sickening fears.'[1] The
words are bare, the phrases grave and entirely simple, as
if crippled by the growing uselessness of saying anything
at all. No sympathy is asked, no audience is envisaged.
Almost every dull, placid observation in the last paragraphs contains a searing pain; but the control is such
that a reader might realize no more than that the tale
is being rounded off in rather tired verse. Only a
watchful exposure will find the quietest phrases—

[1] I am indebted to a fine passage in *Wordsworth: a preliminary survey*, by James
Smith. (*Scrutiny*, 1938).

<blockquote>
at her death
The estate was sold. . . .
</blockquote>

the more poignant for their tiredness. Now the source
for this poise is its still place, the movement away from
human kind towards the inanimate, the insentient, the
stationary, to a strange experience of the Other, which
provided a perspective for a tragic narrative of agricultural doom. In movement, in language, in narrative,
the poem closes by a gradual freezing into immobility;
the unfinished sheepfold is its final image.

Even the finest of Hardy's tragic scenes may seem
theatrical by the side of this; but they convince by the
deep and absorbed tenderness pervading them, and by
the truth of the frame of reference—the particulars of a
way of life; they convince by the fitful power of the
country voices, and by the severe ballad-attitude that
invigorates them. The climax of *The Mayor of Caster-*
bridge comes nearest, perhaps, to the bare record of
suffering unalleviated except by the endurance suffering
itself fosters. There are passages of great emotional power
in the last interview between Henchard and his daughter,
with its dramatic context; the half-articulate dignity of
Henchard's voice is beautifully conveyed. But, much
more, there is the labourer's narrative of Henchard's
last hours, just sufficiently sharpened by a dialect vocabulary to evoke working conditions. Abel Whittle's
delivery reveals unsuspected richness when carefully
studied. Hardy's appreciation of the cottage environment stands behind it; and all the while, the labourer's
rough kindliness holds away at a distance any more sensitive response to the events he retails. His consciousness
of temporary responsibility, his naive pleasure in spinning
out the tale, ring true. So its tragic events seem remote,
yet implications that reach back through the novel surround it. But Whittle's voice is absorbed in the incidents,

not their meaning. And the rude pride and authoritative-
ness of Henchard emerge unrelieved.

> 'I seed en go down street on the night of your worshipful's
> wedding to the lady at yer side, and I thought he looked low
> and faltering. And I followed en over Grey's Bridge, and he
> turned and zeed me, and said 'You go back!' But I followed,
> and he turned again, and said 'Do you hear, sir? Go back!'
> But I zeed that he was low, and I followed on still. . . . Then
> he walked on, and I followed; and he never complained at
> me no more. We walked on like that all night; and in the
> blue o' the morning, when 'twas hardly day, I looked ahead
> o' me, and I zeed that he wambled, and could hardly drag
> along. . . .
> But he didn't gain strength, for you see, ma'am, he
> couldn't eat—no, no appetite at all—and he got weaker;
> and today he died. One of the neighbours have gone to get
> a man to measure him.'

So death is acknowledged and accepted without grave
emotion; and 'one of the neighbours have gone to get a
man to measure him'. We have not the unfinished sheepfold, here, but the human remains, and one of the neighbours, and the labourer's voice.

Hardy notes quietly, in contrast to that competence,
a different response.

> 'Dear me—is that so!' said Farfrae.

He is genteel, unaccustomed to dealing with serious
rural eloquence, or with its failure to gloss. Elizabeth
Jane says nothing. Then we reach the counterpart (if the
analogy may be allowed) to Wordsworth's transfixed
moment, the motionless shepherd by the unfinished
sheepfold. The whole passage moves towards this last
encounter with Henchard, where his human vitality
breaks out of the apparent negation of vitality, death.
He is, symbolically, Agricultural Man; he has suffered
defeat; he leaves no posterity, for his daughter is allied

to the town, to Farfrae. He has died; but his voice comes plainly to the ear, speaking in terms of traditional rural pieties and of social living. Each phrase has his accent, his commanding tone, his curt assurance, his harshness. And here in the presence of death, the imaginative references to a frame of conditions for living and to customary human doings, communicate to the stillness a contradictory stirring of vitality. The weight of the whole novel hammers in each phrase.

> That Elizabeth-Jane Farfrae be not told of my death, or made to grieve on account of me.
> & that I be not bury'd in consecrated ground.
> & that no sexton be asked to toll the bell.
> & that nobody is wished to see my dead body.
> & that no murners walk behind me in my funeral.
> & that no flours be planted on my grave.
> & that no man remember me.
> To this I put my name.
>
> > Michael Henchard.

The two other voices once again express in turn the urban incompetence and the rural strength.

> 'What are we to do?' said Donald. . . . She could not answer distinctly. . . .
> 'But there's no altering—so it must be.'

So it must be is inseparable from the human stirring, the persistence in activity, upon which Hardy's tragic effect turns. The agricultural order towards which his fiction leans, held that possibility of acceptance, without fraud or attitudinizing; therefore, even under apparent doom, he was able to present it in particular and identified ways. The *so it must be* comes as the natural response to the bitterness of life, that sprang from certain conditions for living: so the novels affirm.

The bitterness of life with which Hardy's novels deal is not limited to what the agricultural society itself may

K

have to endure. Hardy had, in Lawrence's phrase, looked out into the wilderness. He was lost, and there could be for him no return; he could not become a simple countryman, and he did not try to. But there has been, the novels say, a facing of despair, of chaos, of purpose-lessness—of all that profound and serious study, and experience of the larger world, revealed. And Hardy's art records as plainly a movement of acceptance, one made valid by the agricultural condition, where a kind of humility and stoicism grows, whose passiveness pro-vides for a contrary persistence in purposeful activity.

A powerful direct projection of this personal conflict comes during the early novel, *A Pair of Blue Eyes*. Knight, holding precariously to the cliff face, looks out into the wilderness, (to continue with Lawrence's phrase) and endures what he sees and experiences, through a humble and stoic acceptance of his creatureliness. His wilder-ness is explicitly related to the revelations of modern knowledge. The cruel and meaningless disaster that leads to the loss of Oak's sheep, and his consequent appearance at the Hiring Fair, provides a similar metaphor —although here the disaster has something of the quality of that series of harsh accidents which during the decade following the appearance of this novel accentuated the tragedy befalling our agriculture: the bad harvests, the ravages of disease. The conditions of which the disaster is part also nourish Oak's strength to persist humbly and dourly in his vocation. The phrases with which Hardy's best biographer described his later years, come to mind:

> While Hardy was impressed with the gathering pheno-mena of grim things to come, he remained sedulous in the minor affairs of life; and he balanced his dismay at certain immense historical generalities with a loving respect for man as a modest, enduring, trusting wayfarer.[1]

[1] E. Blunden: *Thomas Hardy*.

Hardy has quoted in his notebooks an insight learnt in his 'wilderness'. 'Be not perturbed; for everything is according to the universal.' The words are those of Marcus Aurelius. But the voice is the voice of Joan Durbeyfield: 'Tis nater, I suppose, and what do please God. It is the voice of Henchard: I am to suffer, I perceive. It is some unnamed country voice: Your lot is your lot, and Scripture is nothing. It is the voice of Elizabeth-Jane, of one after another of her country folk: 'Twas to be. The tone and the usual context of the affirmation transcend the apparent pessimism. 'Twas to be; and the seasons' return, nature's fecundity, the seed sown and the harvest reaped, all the bounty of earth and the generation of man and beast, are agreed for by the same recognition.

When Troy, in *Far from the Madding Crowd*, reveals to his wife his constant devotion to Fanny Robin,

> . . . there arose from Bathsheba's lips a long, low cry . . . of anguish such as had never before been heard within those old-inhabited walls. It was the τετέλεσται of her union with Troy.

The last phrase, and Hardy's Greek term, remind us how the despair and frustration projected in this crisis of the tale relate to the insights of 'the wilderness'. Bathsheba disappears into the darkness, 'along the dark road, neither knowing nor caring about the direction or issue of her flight'. She finds her way into a wood, and sinks down

> . . . upon a tangled couch of fronds and stems. She mechanically pulled some armfuls round her to keep off the breezes, and closed her eyes.

From disaster in the city of Bath, through acknowledgment of it in 'those old-inhabited walls' to a tangled couch of fronds in the countryside: that is the movement.

But how precarious the restoration feels! Although the
countryside (as elsewhere in Hardy) assumes a kind of
mother-quality, Bathsheba's dream becomes a nightmare
before morning.

The sense of restoration is unmistakable.

> It was with a freshened existence and a cooler brain that,
> a long time afterwards, she became conscious of some
> interesting proceedings which were going on in the trees
> above her head and around.

The movement becomes as surprising as it is delicately
tough. Bathsheba is no more a bird settling to the nest.
The resilient tone marked in the phrase 'interesting
proceedings' controls the whole sequence, a wiry, accurate little drama of the stirrings and the goings-on that
give body to the 'freshened existence'.

> A coarse-throated chatter was the first sound.
> It was a sparrow just waking.
> Next, 'Chee-weeze-weeze-weeze!' from another retreat.
> It was a finch.
> Third, 'Tink-tink-tink-tink-a-chink!' from the hedge.
> It was a robin.
> 'Chuck chuck chuck!' overhead.
> A squirrel.
> Then from the road, 'With my ra-ta-ta, and my rum-tum-
> tum!'
> It was a ploughboy. . . .
> She believed from his voice that he was one of the boys on
> her own farm. He was followed by a shambling tramp of
> heavy feet, and looking through the ferns Bathsheba could
> just discern in the wan light of daybreak a team of her own
> horses.

With the warmth and point of that 'It was a ploughboy',
the passage spreads out its circles to resume the tale.
But the sensuous, highly-charged metaphorical narrative
continues:

> She watched them flouncing into the pool, drinking, toss-
> ing up their heads, drinking again, the water dribbling from
> their lips in silver threads. . . .
> She looked further around. Day was just dawning. . . .
> She perceived that in her lap, and clinging to her hair,
> were red and yellow leaves which had come down from the
> tree and settled silently upon her during her partial sleep. . . .
> There was an opening towards the east, and the glow from
> the as yet unrisen sun attracted her eyes thither.

Then the treacherous swamp reveals itself at the moment
of restoration and of sunrise. We feel the precariousness
of the restoration: the metaphor defines it with strange
intensity. Again we may sense the menace of 'the wilderness'. And then the voice of the schoolboy interrupts,
and the voice of Liddy, and the persisting vitality re-
asserts itself. Bathsheba, Hardy says, 'revived with the
spring' and 'as the summer drew on, she passed more of
her time in the open air, and began to examine into
farming matters from sheer necessity.'

In *Tess of the D'Urbervilles* the expression of Hardy's
stoic theme is more masterful. Book Three, *The Rally*,
suggests the conditions for a healthy, mirthful society able
to restore a Tess overtaken by tragic events or a Clare
beset by 'the ache of modernism'. The farm itself, the
daily round, the voices and physical activities, make
their gradual effect. Tess's hopelessness and dismay give
place to hope and tranquillity. Clare may be thought
to engage Hardy's personal experiences more immediately. Concerning him, the narrative is explicit.

> Early association with country solitudes had bred in him
> an unconquerable, and almost unreasonable, aversion to
> modern town life. . . .

His entry into agricultural society compares closely with
the opening of Hardy's own article, *The Dorsetshire
Labourer*. The explanatory writing about him is clumsy,

but the pressure may be felt. The three girls of balladry, Izz, Marian, and Hetty, and the freshly, sensuously described activities of dairy farming, and the passing of the seasons substantiate the restoration.

The second rally, at Flintcomb Ash, is a yet more powerful image, so adequate to the tension compelling it that the writing becomes supremely moving. It is as though 'the wilderness' were absorbed into the agricultural environment itself; the pain, the hopelessness, the sombre harshness of the life here, speak for themselves. The brutality of the farmer-owner, the girls' reliance on the bottle, the wistful helplessness of the older labourers, have no covering gloss. Yet even these conditions restore, by nourishing the will to persist. The last place I shall point to in this context presents a quieter situation. His capacity for impersonal writing touches heights, here. The narrative absorbs his emotion and completely projects his insight. The passage tells of the Lady Day migrations and of the final calamity for Tess's family that they bring—the source of Tess's own final calamity. The migration is a dark symbol of the disintegration of agricultural life, and the culmination of the series that begins with the hiring-fair of *Far from the Madding Crowd*. Dispossessed and uprooted, like so many labourers and artisans, the Durbeyfields are assisted by their neighbours as they prepare to move. As always, it is the vivid particulars, the details, that reveal the quality of the invention. Packing over, the actual house-ridding gets under way:

> It proceeded with some cheerfulness, a friendly neighbour or two assisting. When the large articles of furniture had been packed in position a circular nest was made of the beds and bedding, in which Joan Durbeyfield and the young children were to sit through the journey. After loading there was a long delay before the horses were brought,

these having been unharnessed during the ridding; but at length, about two o'clock, the whole was under way, the cooking-pot swinging from the axle of the waggon, Mrs. Durbeyfield and family at the top, the matron having in her lap, to prevent injury to its works, the head of the clock, which, at any exceptional lurch of the waggon, struck one, or one-and-a-half, in hurt tones.

Let this be considered in its context of distress, the personal distress occasioned by the narrative, and the other deep distress occasioned by the significance of such migrations in the agricultural world, and one is struck by the curious buoyancy of feeling in the language. The impartiality verges on the carefree, yet there are keen, painful sensations at work, and one knows it. The preparations are so orderly, everything is done imperturbably, though the *nest* of beds and bedding contains a tiny shaft of pathos; the swinging cooking-pot touches the scene with an uncanny jollity. And, if anywhere, the peculiar verve crystallizes here: *the matron having on her lap, to prevent injury to its works, the head of the clock which, at any exceptional lurch, struck one, or one-and-a-half, in hurt tones.* One hears those tones, their muffled oddity. This is like Dickens at the height of his powers, and there is nothing higher in English fiction.

The pages that follow are nearly as fine; but here, pointedly enough, is the strange co-presence of incompatibles, of disturbance and distress on the one hand, and buoyant imperturbability on the other. The fiction locks together the component elements of Hardy's deepest experience, the dismay of the wilderness, and the persisting strength of the enclosed agricultural communities.

The storm symbols in the novels serve to dramatize these incompatibles, the dismay and the steadfastness.

Again and again Hardy constructs an image of human persistence in strength of purpose under the stress of some storm, some unleashing of natural rigours. Knight's experience in *A Pair of Blue Eyes* is one occasion; Oak and Bathsheba thatching and binding beneath the lightning and the rain is the most famous. Storms twice defeat Henchard's purposes, and prolonged rain and eventual storm brings Giles Winterborne to his death through unfaltering devotion to 'the smaller morality' of the enclosed community. Very likely the calamitous harvests of 1874–9 left some such impress as this upon Hardy's imagination, and *The Mayor of Casterbridge* seems particularly to testify to them. But *Far from the Madding Crowd*, at least, had already appeared. The image is partly of Hardy's own contrivance.

The harsh season at Flintcomb Ash is a sort of culmination to this series, and the most moving of all. But each instance serves to focus a resistant human steadfastness. Hardy did not needlessly idealize it. His own quiet attempt at a definition comes by way of a private comment on the action of *The Woodlanders*:

> The trees dripped on the garden plots where no vegetables would grow for the dripping, though they were planted year after year, *with that curious mechanical regularity of country people in the face of hopelessness.*

The fullest adumbration forms part of the important article on *The Dorsetshire Labourer*. The passage is too often quoted without its corollary.

> Wherever a mode of supporting life is neither noxious nor absolutely inadequate, there springs up happiness and will spring up happiness of some sort or another. Indeed, it is among communities such as these that happiness will find her last refuge upon earth, for it is among them that perfect insight into the conditions of existence will be longest postponed. . . . Drudgery in the slums and alleys

of a city, too long pursued, and accompanied as it is by
indifferent health, may induce a mood of despondency
well-nigh permanent. But the same degree of despondency
in the fields results at worst in a mood of painless passivity.

There is the observer's drab formulation. But the tension between dismay and steadfastness, and the perception of the conditions of life that nourish the steadfastness, together compose the very substance of the
novelist's art.

'The essential function of art is moral', wrote D. H.
Lawrence. 'Not aesthetic, not decorative, not recrea-
tional, not pastime, but moral.' It is so. In what
measure, then, are Hardy's best novels a criticism of *life*?
From what profundity of experience do they derive, and
with what stirring or disquieting truth is that experience
ordered and recorded? In what measure are we altered,
quickened to fresh insight, moved to new levels of sensitiveness, troubled where the consciousness lay dormant?
It seems right, by way of conclusion, to attempt some
answer, albeit a personal, limited, and tentative answer.

The novels may be taken, first, as a record of a tragic
view of life. One cannot but respond to the strong simplicity and integrity of Hardy's feeling, to its consistency,
its 'Franciscan tenderness', its unforced compassion.[1] To
read and reflect upon the imaginative fictions contrived
by those qualities, controlled by a stern insight, and set
down with strenuous honesty of purpose, does indeed
touch and chasten the spirit. I believe the power so to
chasten and subdue, to be the essential value of the
novels. And the profounder perturbation of spirit, the
experience we associate with the encounter with the
greatest tragic art? Save for certain precarious moments,
that is out of reach. The total tragic invention, in

[1] I am indebted to a passage from a review by Q. D. Leavis.

Hardy, does not so stir us, is not of the sort to communicate the profoundest insights or the profoundest qualm,
as Conrad's is, or D. H. Lawrence's. We are subdued;
but we have not made radical questioning of our present sufficiencies. We have been deliberately reminded,
but not made profoundly aware, of the darker order of
things. There are limits to Hardy's power, limits connected with the pressure of nostalgia upon his art, and
with the inflexibility of his nature. The novels have
moments of sudden, even astonishing, tragic suggestion;
but these remain moments only. The total structures do
not draw out, develop or enforce the suggestion; nor do
they measure and comprehend the tragedy.

The secondary strength of Hardy's fiction resides in its
power to quicken apprehension of the quality and value
of life in the agricultural community, with its traditional
ways and faith. Hardy communicates his feeling for this
quality, and its historical predicament, in a vital relation with his stern convictions about human vicissitudes.
Be it admitted that the urgency that informs the novelist's
valuation of the agricultural order partakes of nostalgia; there is little place for the costly impersonality
of unalloyed artistic vision. Wessex is moulded, in a
measure, by the stress of Hardy's personal needs; he
himself called it, in his first intention, his 'dream
country'. But (in his own expressive phrase) 'it solidi-
fied.' His longing found satisfaction in a definite agricultural community and environment, and submitted to
their facts. Wessex is not merely a simplified world, and
such simplicity as it has may not lightly be dismissed.
Let Hardy be compared with the original and unduly
neglected Richard Jefferies. The latter's essays and
sketches, and above all *The Dewy Morn* and *Amaryllis at
the Fair*, his two most impressive novels, should have
their permanent place alongside Hardy's novels on our

shelves. Of rural truth we shall discover less in Hardy's Wessex than in Jefferies's Wiltshire, for Jefferies had the more penetrating knowledge of the whole range of agricultural life, the more passionate sympathy with the labourers, by far the surer grasp of rural economics, and the more astonishing sensibility towards the natural environment. The insight, the candour, the modesty and the sensuousness of his prose, and the strange audacity of some strokes of invention in his narratives, lay bare a sort of poverty in all but the finest pages of Hardy.[1]

For all that, very likely we shall take down the great Wessex novels more often. Their tragic tenor apart, they still have qualities sufficient to compensate for any poverty, qualities for which we shall go in vain to Jefferies. We cannot *know* Wessex as we can Wiltshire; nor will even Oak affect us quite as Iden can. But Hardy's agricultural documentaries have their own massive cogency. Take them as a sustained imagery of agricultural calamity, and Jefferies's work appears sketchy and fragmentary in comparison. Hardy remains unique for the searching relevance of his stories to his agricultural testimony. Moreover, the traditional basis of his narrative art lends it a strength denied to Jefferies. In the extreme force and the guileless fascination of his narrative, Hardy yields to no master in our language. His finest are indeed tales which hold children from play and old men from the chimney corner. They have done so already for half a century and more, and there is no sign that their strange power diminishes with time.

[1] The classic account of Jefferies is to be found in Edward Thomas's critical biography—by far the best introduction to his work. Of the two authors' treatment of agricultural labourers, Thomas pertinently remarks: 'Jefferies does not go far with them . . . but his handling is absolutely sympathetic and understanding. Mr. Hardy is far more dramatic, far more psychological, and also far cleverer in effects, but he is seldom so right.'

THE HARVEST OF THE NOVELS

I

'Now *there* is a clarity. There *is* the harvest of having written 20 novels first.' So Mr. Ezra Pound wrote of Hardy's *Collected Poems*—the italics are his. For the letter of the matter he is inaccurate: not all even of the best poetry was composed after the novels. But for the spirit, he is profoundly just. And his tribute to Hardy's impact is the more notable because he has paid due tribute to Browning as well. One suspects that some poets who claim to have owed so much to Hardy are in some measure also speaking of a debt to Browning of which they are either unaware or a little ashamed. In spite of deep differences from him, Hardy himself studied Browning's verse intently and with admiration. The novelist's poetry has been the medium through which Browning's bold, if sometimes coarse, reconstruction of a vernacular poetic idiom became useful to twentieth-century poets. They, and we, think first of Hardy because, whatever he learnt from Browning, the mode of his speech was more embracing, more gentle, less apt to strike an attitude, more thorough and dour in its acknowledgement of the contemporary world, more candid.

Hardy has in fact been a profound force in modern poetry. 'Nobody has taught me anything about writing since Thomas Hardy died,' said Mr. Pound in another letter; and elsewhere, though he wanted people to be able to penetrate the sham and the falsified, he added, 'It is only maturer patience that can sweep aside a writer's honest error, and overlook unaccomplished clumsiness, or outlandishness, or old-fashionedness, for the sake of the solid centre. Thus many people have overlooked Thomas Hardy's verses, even though the author of *The Mayor of Casterbridge* lurks behind them.' The novelist is indeed behind them, serious, compassionate, distressed by the blindness of chance, curiously aware of impotence, and deeply concerned for a particular community. The character of the man is there too: gentle, magnanimous, unaffectedly simple in his sense of great issues, and capable of very deep feeling.

The solid centre, the clarity: there we have Hardy's personal note in poetry, that direct, unequivocal report upon unreserved experience. At the same time, Mr. Pound's emphasis on the value for the poet of the years spent in writing the novels is a useful corrective. Hardy's profound discomfort as a novelist, and the unhappiness that clouded his final achievements, together with the revelation in the last novel that there was no more he could *do* as a novelist, that his art was insufficient for his experience, conspired to make his renunciation of novel-writing over-emphatic. True, he was a poet first, and continued practising his poetry throughout those years; and when he was able, in the later years, to devote all his energies to the poet's vocation, he achieved in poetry a distinction as unique as any he achieved in fiction. But we should not be misled by his occasional and bitter derogation of his achievement as a novelist. The composition of the important novels, which Hardy himself unerringly identified when preparing the *Collected Edition*, terming them *Novels of Character and Environment*, was a careful labour of art and a contribution to the training of a poet. It helped him to know profoundly what he was interested in, where his mind and imagination and passional nature worked freely. There, in one style of art, he discovered those situations of the spirit he could best identify and celebrate in verse: situations of longing and of loss, of nostalgia and of transitoriness. There, too, he formulated his simple acknowledgement of elementary sanctions, his acquiescence in the impassive or alien nature of the human environment as it appeared to him, his respect for a stoicism nourished by the conditions of agricultural life. He never ceased, as a poet, to draw upon those formulations. The poetry *is* the 'harvest of the novels'.

It is indeed a harvest. The matter of bulk is not important. Granted that he lived long, Hardy was still prolific; and it is true that numberless pieces offer something of interest, some touch of odd eloquence, some indication of personal idiosyncrasy; true that this continual practice of the poet's art was necessary, necessary to keep a channel clear and flowing. But Hardy's claim to poetic stature rests upon a very small collection of poems, drawn from all his volumes. His loss has been that readers of poetry have not as yet been presented with a small enough collection of his very richest work, a collection including some few pieces representing the variety of his achievement, but comprising chiefly the dramatic and lyrical elegies. Such a collection, freshly approached, might still astonish many. And although some poems of Hardy's earlier years would find a place there, the poetry of the later years, when Hardy was free to concentrate all his resources upon the vocation of his earliest choice, would predominate.

During Wind and Rain may be taken to represent very clearly all that is most personal, unusual, and strong, in his poetry. It is an elegy.

They sing their dearest songs-—
He, she, all of them—yea,
Treble and tenor and bass,
    And one to play;
With the candles mooning each face. . . .
    Ah, no; the years O!
How the sick leaves reel down in throngs!

They clear the creeping moss—
Elders and juniors—aye,
Making the pathways neat
    And the garden gay;
And they build a shady seat. . . . .
    Ah, no; the years, the years;
See, the webbed white storm-birds wing across.

They are blithely breakfasting all—
Men and maidens—yea,
Under the summer tree,
    With a glimpse of the bay,
While pet fowl come to the knee. . . . .
    Ah, no; the years O!
And the rotten rose is ript from the wall.

They change to a high new house,
He, she, all of them—aye,
Clocks and carpets and chairs
    On the lawn all day,
And brightest things that are theirs. . . .
    Ah, no; the years, the years;
Down their chiselled names the rain-drop ploughs.

We seem to have there the elements of a modest, somewhat trite and indulgent expression of the mood of regret. The memories have no distinction or force of their own, yet no gesture of eloquence claims anything for them that might make up for their ordinariness. We have to take back that 'indulgent expression' because things are offered so unaffectedly; the very triviality of

the scenes, too slight to elicit a profound sense of loss,
vouches for a truthfulness that has no designs upon us.
The gentle, singing lines of the quatrain in each verse
hold unexpected exactness, and the fifth line tacks on
the remembered detail with a sort of wide-awake shyness. The memories, instead of blurring in a haze of
regret, seem to come clearly and immediately upon the
consciousness, unsought after. The details are domestic,
social, unpretentious and unapologetic.

> Treble and tenor and bass,
>   And one to play;
>
> Making the pathways neat. . . .

—breakfasting under a tree; moving furniture. One
feels, considering just the opening of each verse, that the
memories are distinct and active of their own accord,
returning upon the poet as if uninvited; and by him
quietly checked, so as not to intrude upon others, advancing claims for sympathy.

One examines these deceptively simple quatrains
afresh, and they extend themselves in the mind, taking
on a seasonal rhythm. The present moment is in the
wind and rain, and there is winter in the first memory,
and the human intimacy of the closed home circle making music. Each memory responds to a situation of human
activity, and has a kind of warmth inside itself. But how
subtly coloured the winter memory is,

> With the candles *mooning* each face,

and how characteristic the word-coinage: the noun is
pressed into activity as a verb, and the candles make the
picture of each face, encircled by blackness, flicker and
move. But the ashen-yellow moon colour divests them
of the glow and freshness of music-making; they have
at once the curious remoteness of memory about them.

L

Then comes spring, with its domestic preparations for out-door days, and summer, with a glimpse away from home and towards the sea, and a suggestion of growth— the children have grown up. The repeated verbal movements, the rhythmical echoes and variations between the stanzas, reinforce the sense of the seasonal round. The autumn memory (so to call it, for nothing so definite is stated) gives to transience an image of its own—moving house.

Evidently the song-like air, the accurate run of domestic detail, register the unforced passage of memories through the mind—a mind acquiescent because it accords with seasonal change and renewal. We are at first bemused because the poetic art appears to claim so little. But what more significance those memories do hold, the marvellous break into another movement, another style of song at the end of each verse, brings home. It is his power to juxtapose a desolate present with an incompatible, intruding past, that distinguishes Hardy. Here, as if stirred by the broken refrain of some half-remembered song, the poetry comes painfully to a consciousness of the present moment during wind and rain. At the same time, the pause of the lilting quatrain, the tentative stretch of the 5th line, are also interrupted by the very sound and gesture of a speaking voice: ah no; ah no. And again, his power to use dramatically the natural inflexions of speech distinguishes Hardy.

With the quiet vocal gesture there is preserved the folk-song lilt (or so, at least, I read it), and in alternate stanzas the repeated words hold back the onward impulse, oppressing with the weight of recollection.

> Ah, no; the years, the years;

These refrains seem to carry a social endorsement. As song-refrains, they recollect the way many men and women in all ages have found things to be. With that

'Ah, no', personal grief has to take its place alongside everyone else's; there is a sombre season in the human condition, and there are other seasons too. The recognition is neither indignant nor grandiloquent. It just flowers, opens up naturally out of the juxtaposition of then and now, both so definitely present. We are drawn to appreciate, in such verse, a human spirit trained in clear, unfuddled response to experience.

That recognition is behind the poetic art of the last line of each stanza. The broken refrain is not left to speak for itself; it releases a series of dramatic perceptions, imaginary extensions of this present moment, enacted in a rhythm heavy and drawn-out with the weight of regret and pain of acknowledgement. Here the desolation between wind and rain, the incipient winter, are perpetual; but the feeling is more than personal . The lines have the bold folklore suggestiveness of balladry.

> How the sick leaves reel down in throngs!

> See, the webbed white storm-birds wing across.

> And the rotten rose is ript from the wall.

Yet with each culminating line the feeling and movement are different. The faintly debilitating interest in decay (the sick leaves and the rotten rose) is checked by watchfulness and stamina: the *white* birds *winging*, the rose *ript* from the wall. These lines come upon the mind with overtones of universal diminishing, falling away, grieving; but there is also a feeling for seasonal return, freshness and growth as well as change and loss. The birds are white, the rose tree is pruned for new growths. Delicately, in the last line of all, the one implicit statement of the deaths, these strands of feeling and acquiescence all unite:

> Down their chiselled names the rain-drop ploughs.

Each earlier perception seems now to have foreshadowed this one. Yet, regretful as they are, these last words bring rain to the roots (the rain of the present moment) and the last metaphor is of the plough.

This is still to do less than justice to the poetry of that last stanza, where the memory of the house-moving prepares so gently for the recognition of death. But the rough analysis serves to indicate the sort of power we are to look for in Hardy's elegiac verse, and to identify the sources of his strength. Certainly the hiding-places of his power, as with Wordsworth, were in the past. But the particular poetic sources are these: a vital relation with traditional music, folksong and balladry; a sombre feeling for the transience and the intermittent bitterness of the human lot, for the necessity of suffering, drawn from the truthfulness of Hardy's own acceptances, from his nostalgia, and from the simple, generous wisdom he brought to bear—from what Middleton Murry so excellently called 'the deliberate purity of his responsiveness;'[1] a peculiar flair for catching the timbre of the perceived 'moment' and for recording a sudden profundity of sensation; and a unique quality of elegiac feeling responsive to the poignancy of incident returning unsought upon the unguarded memory, and released through dramatic fantasy.

Any collection of Hardy's most distinguished verse would contain some few poems where these four sources suggest themselves strongly and independently of each other, as well as the finest elegies. This essay is now to treat briefly of these successes: a few pieces of folk verse and narrative balladry; some poems of meditation or statement directly expressing the poet's response to his environment, and his grave view of life, or the exiled countryman's nostalgia; some more frag-

[1] 'The Poetry of Thomas Hardy' in *Aspects of Literature* (1919).

mentary pieces evoking the immediate 'moment' whose significance trembles and eludes. It may be possible, then, to appreciate more adequately the achievement of the elegies, where the separate strengths blend together to constitute the singular triumphs of Hardy's poetic genius. By dint of those triumphs he is a major poet, and this in spite of his artistic conservatism (he envisaged, he said, no new paths in poetry), his Victorian certainties and uncertainties, and in spite of a poetic equipment quite extraordinarily assorted: including alongside such strengths as we have already noted, the bardic manner, poeticisms, the rustic and the colloquial, the gauche and the prosaic, inflexibility, ingenuity, candour.

II

IT is best to begin with the folk songs, the balladry and the narratives. Even the best poems in this group may well be thought inferior; but this starting place reminds us of the true genesis of Hardy's poetic art—in the music of his youth, in the ballads still known and sung in the Wessex of his boyhood. The most cursory glance over the *Collected Poems*, or through the pages of his life story, reveals Hardy's deep feeling for music. In part this feeling may derive from an association in his mind and memory between music-making and the Wessex communities of his boyhood. Here is the source of Hardy's 'singing' line, which was not at all a matter of skilful verbal euphony. Though Hardy was assiduous in metrical practice and experiment, and in the pursuit of novel prosodic effects, though he filled abstract verse-patterns with sounds and stresses, the labours brought few striking successes. His most moving rhythmical effects respond more directly to the pressures of experience; they do not come from the study of metrics. They occur with simplicity and verve, sudden modifications of a singing

pattern, unforgettable alterations of weight. They derive
from the special relation in his art between the rhythms
and tunes of folk song and balladry (which are not necessarily simple) and his studied immersion in the tradition
of English poetry, especially in the verse of Browning and
Barnes.

The same situation illuminates the diction of his verse.
For the achievement of his poetic language, too, he
worked hard, studied widely and carefully, revised
severely (up to a point; but he would not risk the poem's
losing its 'freshness', he said,) and usually felicitously.
Yet the result is improvisatory; the assimilation of the
various elements is quite incomplete. There are few
poems of his whose language is untarnished. The shafting
phrases go alongside so much muffled verbal idiosyncrasy.
But if a common source exists, we should seek it in the
diction of nineteenth-century country balladry, a language
at once conventional, harsh, direct, colloquial and un-
lovely. Not that Hardy constructed a language for modern
balladry: the idiomatic Dorsetshire after Barnes, the
archaic phrase, the Swinburnian rhythm and alliteration,
the pedantic or the grotesque, the delicate or the abrupt
vernacular term, the Shakespearean manner, and the cor-
rugated verbal surface after Browning, jostle too uneasily
side by side, made often interesting, sometimes over-
powering, by the determination of spirit that bent such
miscellaneous ingredients to its poetic purposes.

The ballads, and the light folk verse in the vein of
Weathers, illuminate the movement and diction of Hardy's
finer poetry; but they have originalities of their own.
They indicate most clearly the vivid sense of time and
place that pervades all his poetry. The best of his Wessex
ballads are akin to the best parts of the novels and short
stories in their feel of 'local hearts and heads'. Their
irony is not fickle any more than it is subtle. There is

weight behind it, as of whole communities who have
found life such and such to encounter.

Their imagery is local and domestic, their movement
often dramatic and effective. Take *Her Death and After*,
one of the finest. Hardy learnt much from Browning in
the conduct of verse narrative; but this he learnt from
no one:

> And there, as I paused by her tenement,
> And the trees shed on me their rime and hoar,
> I thought of the man who had left her lone,
>> Him who made her his own
> When I loved her, long before.

> The rooms within had the piteous shine
> That home-things wear when there's aught amiss;
> From the stairway floated the rise and fall
>> Of an infant's call,
> Whose birth had brought her to this.

Nor did he learn such a transition of rhythm under the
impress of imagery, as follows the woman's dying request.

> —When I had left, *and the swinging trees*
>> *Rang above me*, as lauding her candid say,
>> Another was I . . .

Friends Beyond represents a more familiar style of popular
verse, and it is specially distinguished for the vivid feeling
of a real and local past, inhabited by a human community,
and for the attitude towards death, lightly enough indicated here, that is constant in Hardy's best verse. 'It
is in the contemplation of death,' Dr. I. A. Richards has
said, speaking of Hardy's poetry, 'that the necessity for
human attitudes to become self-supporting in the face of
an indifferent universe, is felt most poignantly. Only the
greatest tragic poets have achieved an equally self-reliant
and immitigable acceptance.'[1]

[1] I. A. Richards: *Science and Poetry* (1926).

William Dewy, Tranter Reuben, Farmer Ledlow late at
      plough,
    Robert's kin, and John's, and Ned's,
And the Squire, and Lady Susan, lie in Mellstock churchyard
      now!

'Gone,' I call them, gone for good, that group of local
      hearts and heads;
    Yet at mothy curfew-tide,
And at midnight when the noon-heat breathes it back from
      walls and leads,

They've a way of whispering to me—fellow-wight who yet
      abide—
    In the muted, measured note
Of a ripple under archways, or a lone cave's stillicide:

'We have triumphed: this achievement turns the bane to
      antidote,
    Unsuccesses to success,
Many thought-worn eves and morrows to a morrow free of
      thought.

No more need we corn and clothing, feel of old terrestrial
      stress;
    Chill detraction stirs no sigh;
Fear of death has even bygone us: death gave all that we
      possess. . . .'

The moralized treatment of mutability would count for
little, were it not infused with so actual a recollected
past, vouched for by the strains and pressures in the
curious verbal coinages and arrangements reporting a
tough pre-occupation with objects and facts, the Barnes-
ian hyphenates—thought-worn, curfew-tide—and the
arresting movement, constantly varying, its lingering
reminiscent lines tightened by the short-breathed lines
between.

Such a poem as *Channel Firing* also remains close

to the local narrative and supernatural mode of this balladry. Its tune alters surprisingly as the poem develops, and the changing rhythms enact the alterations with deliberate verve. Perhaps Hardy's best achievement in the true irony of the country ballad is *The Turnip Hoer*, but the essence of his skill in balladry and light verse has gone into *The Dead Quire*. Here is the hard centre of controlled nostalgia, a profound awareness of lost stabilities and certainties, and a mordant humour insinuating actuality into time and place and person. It is a naïve country tale of the old choir, long dead and buried, whose voices are heard singing the old Christmas hymn on Christmas Eve. The memory has for Hardy a personal resonance. Here, in the ballad, it invests the present hauntingly with the past and its compulsive claim upon deep-seated allegiances. How the discrepant parts of Hardy's poetic speech fuse together in this:

> The singers had followed one by one,
> Treble, and tenor, and thorough-bass;
> And the worm that wasteth had begun
> To mine their mouldering place. . . .

The singing quality of the opening lines, and their staple idiom gives place to the biblical phraseology Hardy had known so familiarly in his youth, and then the feeling for old sanctities is gently modified by the grim accuracy of *mine*, and the *mouldering place*, slightly grotesque, a mental arrangement all Hardy's own. Then with what finesse he gives the supernatural occasion locality and moment:

> Then did the Quick pursue the Dead
> By crystal Froom that crinkles there;
> And still the viewless quire ahead
> Voiced the old holy air.

By Bank-walk wicket, brightly bleached,
It passed, and 'twixt the hedges twain
Dogged by the living; till it reached
    The bottom of Church Lane.

There, at the turning, it was heard
Drawing to where the Churchyard lay:
But when they followed thitherward
    It smalled, and died away.

Each headstone of the quire, each mound,
Confronted them beneath the moon;
But no more floated therearound
    That ancient Birth-night tune.

The Oxen is a more famous folk song in precisely the
vein of *The Dead Quire*. Hardy is always singularly
effective when he closes his verses in gloom, twilight,
or darkness.

       Yet, I feel,
   If someone said on Christmas Eve,
     'Come; see the oxen kneel

   In the lonely barton by yonder coomb
    Our childhood use to know',
   I should go with him in the gloom,
    Hoping it might be so.

The simplicity is not factitious; it springs from a genuine
simplicity that is part of the poet's own nature.

These notes do not exhaust Hardy's successes in
balladry. There are more thoroughly colloquial pieces,
for instance, after the style of Barnes: *The Bride-Night
Fire* has a thrust beyond what pastiche can achieve.
And any list would include the famous *The Trampwoman's
Tragedy*, which was among Hardy's own favourites, *The
Woman in the Rye*, *In the Servants' Quarters*, *The Rash
Bride*, and *The Choirmaster's Funeral*. They may not be
great poems, but they are the work of a remarkable

practitioner in this mode. And he can adapt the mode to a more personal kind of experience, as in the lovely *When I set out for Lyonesse*. There, the fusion of the tune and style of light folk verse with a deep personal emotion points towards his greatest lyrical achievements. On the other hand, a poem like the grim and impressive *The Souls of the Slain* seems to belong rather to Hardy's own readings of life; but it is from balladry that it draws its vitality. Indeed, this that I have designated the folk verse and the ironic balladry is not a strict category but a style that permeates all his best verse, as it permeates, for instance, *Drummer Hodge*. To start with some poems such as those mentioned here establishes in the mind and ear a proper readiness.

III

WE turn to the group of poems that record with more directness Hardy's readings of life, his assessments of experience, his sense of the contemporary world; and with them we should consider some verse that presents, without the thread or covering of the ballad story, his nostalgia, and his relation to contemporary Wessex. These poems are only readings of life, as Hardy insisted. He endeavoured no general or consistent philosophy; his business, he conceived, was with integrity of response. The consistency we do discover is a consistency of character. 'He is the poet who has most steadily refused to be comforted in an age in which the temptation to seek comfort has been greatest. The comfort of forgetfulness, the comfort of beliefs, he has put both these away.'[1] The weight, the inward gravity, and above all the *deliberate* recognition of nature's indifference to the human plight make these poems, even the slighter of them, impressive. *In Time of the Breaking*

[1] I. A. Richards: *Science and Poetry* (1926).

of Nations takes us straight to the perpetual centre
of the vision Hardy's art contains; the experience it
turns upon was forty years within him before he composed the poem. So momentous a perception could
hardly be more unassumingly versed. It is as firm and
equable as *The Lacking Sense* is insecure in its projection
of the incompatibility of the remote, unconcerned, alien
natural environment with the acute sensitiveness of its
creatures. Yet, 'Thou art of her clay,' that poem ends,
and many of Hardy's distressed readings of life acknow-
ledge it. The gentle gravity is common equally to both
poems.

The tone of these readings is not defeatist. Rather it
is indicated in the conclusion of *The Sleep-Worker*. Should
nature awaken to percipience—

> Should that morn come, and show thy opened eyes
> All that Life's palpitating tissues feel,
> How wilt thou bear thyself in thy surprise?—
>
> Wilt thou destroy, in one wild shock of shame,
> Thy whole high heaving firmamental frame,
> Or patiently adjust, amend, and heal?

Nature's Questioning, *At a Lunar Eclipse*, *To an Unborn
Pauper Child*—these are characteristic poems of the kind
I have in mind here. In the best of them, like this last,
the poetry persuades by its blending of some particular
and local occasion unobtrusively into general reflection.
Hardy's usual note of patient hope sounds out more
obtrusively in the celebrated *The Darkling Thrush*. At
first the statement of desolation and incompatibility
seems over-grimly emphatic; nothing in the first stanza
or the opening of the second prepares one for so poignant
a conclusion. Indeed, the poem works partly through
the odd alliance of such formidable speech with so singing

a melodic line. The style is one of slow talk, each word separating itself out meaningfully:

> The ancient pulse of germ and birth
>   Was shrunken hard and dry,
> And every spirit upon earth
>   Seemed fervourless as I.

Suddenly it releases its thread of easy melody, alongside that of the bird:

> At once a voice burst forth among
>   The bleak twigs overhead
> In a full-hearted evensong
>   Of joy illimited.

Then you have the odd alliance so exactly:

> An aged thrush, frail, gaunt, and small,
>   In blast-beruffled plume,
> Had chosen thus to fling his soul
>   Upon the growing gloom.

All the usual elements of Hardy's poetic art conspire here towards magic: the sense of the actual occasion in time and place, the darkening into gloom, the quality of song, the hard resistance to an alien universe. Aware as he is of the bitter incompatibility of human sensitiveness with the natural environment, that very sensitiveness allies him intimately with the creatures, and induces generous and shrewd perceptions of their life. This is the personal situation behind that inspired and moving passage in *The Dynasts*, the scene at nightfall on the eve of Waterloo. Two beautiful descriptions in prose enclose the choric verses, where the deep sense of discrepancy, the acknowledgement of distant impartiality in nature, the acutely sensitive feeling towards the creatures of earth and air, and the unforced regret for the bitter destiny of individual sentient men covered by deepening

gloom, fit together in a singing meditation. And a like
warmth of feeling for tree, grass, plant and flower ani-
mates the delicate song, *A Backward Spring*. Indeed, this
part of Hardy's verse may be called a poetry of discrepancy. The famous line from one of his earliest poems,

> Crass casualty obstructs the sun,

defines the note with an anger that faded with the years.
When all is said and done, however, very few poems of
this kind stand among his best. His strength as a poet
lies elsewhere.

The resolute and genuine quality of Hardy's conception of the bitterness inherent in the human condition
made it possible for him, given the tragic theme, to
write public poetry of no mean order: *The Convergence
of the Twain* (*Lines on the loss of the 'Titanic'*) and, though
it is less fine, *And there was a Great Calm* (*On the signing of
the Armistice, November 11th, 1918*). At the other extreme,
the truly personal statements are gentle and unassertive,
like *He never expected Much* or the celebrated *Afterwards*.
There seems, it may be, little enough perceptible distinction about the poem. Yet one knows, reading it,
that this movement, the music of this utterance, have
already almost a legendary ring; that a poetic personality
of strange originality resides in the very first words:

> When the Present has latched its postern behind
>   my tremulous stay. . . .

The language is inimitable, an alteration of English
poetry. And set against the picture of Hardy we are
often taught to take into our minds, it is strangely gentle
and tender, this poem. There is another little poem of
personal statement worth quoting here, not only for its
economy, but because it may remind us of the emotional
virility, the prolonged life of the senses and the passions,

that were Hardy's, continuing alongside the 'adamantine honesty of soul' that has more often been perceived.

> I look into my glass,
> And view my wasting skin,
> And say, 'Would God it came to pass
> My heart had shrunk as thin!'
>
> For then, I, undistrest
> By hearts grown cold to me,
> Could lonely wait my endless rest
> With equanimity.
>
> But Time, to make me grieve,
> Part steals, lets part abide;
> And shakes this fragile frame at eve
> With throbbings of noontide.

The Impercipient makes us aware of a similarly gentle, disenchanted, but still troubled self present at a Cathedral Service. The desolate little utterances that break up the final lines anticipate the effects of Hardy's masterpieces.

> Enough. As yet disquiet clings
> About us. Rest shall we.

The hymn tune which sings its way through the poem seems at that point to have existed especially to impart a sense of pain to the faltering.

Last in this group, there are the poems in which nostalgia is the decisive emotion; least important for their intrinsic worth, but at their best an indispensable expression of Hardy's character and situation. This is among the pressures canalized in the finest of his elegiac poems. The nostalgic emotion sings itself readily into remembered hymn and song tunes. The rhythm becomes more relaxed, more predictable; the poetry is less disturbed by those eccentricities of idiom, movement and diction that

bring us directly into touch with the iron in Hardy's
spirit. Through the *Collected Poems* the mood is persistent: 'Slip back, Time. . . . Heard no more again, far
or near. . . . Time's unflinching rigour. . . . What's this
that Time is doing unto me? . . . And never again. . . .'
These phrases, and the recurrent invocations of Time
under manifold guises, indicate the strain. But a few of
these poems of nostalgia have a naturalness and an appeal
of their own. *Wessex Heights* sings the mood more
expressively than any other; it is, of course, a dramatic
poem, a reading of experience and not a personal avowal.
But one can hardly doubt the personal tremor. The home,
the shelter reached for, is real equally in the local places
named, and in the release from stresses and from feelings
of insufficiency described so directly. In *Regret not me*,
again, a sentimental emotion is checked by the validity
of its accidents: the seasonal round of Wessex life, the
autumnal fruitfulness. 'Hardy was a countryman,' Dr.
Leavis has said, 'and his brooding mind stayed itself
habitually upon the simple pieties, the quiet rhythms
and the immemorial ritual of rustic life.'[1] Down there,
in the urban environment, the poet of *Wessex Heights* seems

> . . . to be false to myself, to my simple self that was,

and one or two effective poems besides the celebrated
The Oxen express primarily the desire for some less
complex experience of life, for the earlier simplicities
of faith and insight now out of reach for ever. Such are
Afternoon Service at Mellstock, *In Tenebris III*, and *Night: The
Old House*. But it is still the way the first and last of these
start out of particular experiences, the way the emotion
is tied to place and clock, that impart strength to the verse.

> They come and seat them around in their *mouldy* places. . . .

The shrewd term seems to vouch for a wiriness in the
feeling quite at odds with the easiness of the movement.

[1] F. R. Leavis: *New Bearings in English Poetry* (1932).

On an Invitation to the United States, where the poetry turns upon a past strangely invested with graveyard qualities, has a sort of stifled dignity about it that is affecting. But even here, when life has bared its bones to the poet, and ancestry seems all, the place of refuge has an incompatible human warmth attached to it. It is so again in the verses called *In a Wood*. The lilting hymn-tune character of the movement, the indulgence of the mood, cross purposes with the open-eyed acknowledgements and the unaffected determination.

> Heart-halt and spirit-lame
> City-opprest,
> Unto this wood I came
> As to a nest;
> Dreaming that sylvan peace
> Offered the harrowed ease—
> Nature a soft release
> From men's unrest.

But the refusal to deny experience disturbs the mood. The wood appears alien, and not without its own harrowing laws. So the last verse turns to humankind, to the agricultural society, as does the related novel, *The Woodlanders*.

To His Father's Violin reminds us once more of Hardy's personal situation, and in striking fashion. Here, more than ever, appear the materials for sentimentality, and yet the poem reads quite differently. The spasmodic movement fits the recollecting mind. The music-making occasions are part of the essential substance of the Wessex life of Hardy's youth. The setting includes the characteristic nostalgic glimmer and gloom:

> . . . in the blind
> Still profound
> Of the night-time. . . .

M

but the references and the memories are innocently themselves, with no masks or disguises, no blur at the edges.
And the recollected quality, recorded without pretence,
both gives character to this nostalgic poetry, and suggests
its potentialities for some more adequate vision of life.

IV

THERE is, in the *Collected Poems*, some memorable verse
evocative of the sharply perceived 'moment', verse that
sometimes loses its quality immediately, under the burden
of reflection. Some small, poignant dramatic studies
after Browning's manner—but differently resolved—
like *In the Study*, or *In a Waiting Room*, reveal a natural
evocative gift. Hardy has a flair for the searching, scour-
ing little phrase:

> He enters, and mute on the edge of a chair
> Sits a thin-faced lady, a stranger there,
> A type of decayed gentility. . . .

The sudden, effective openings that distinguish so many
of the shorter poems speak for the same poetic impulse:
to take the very feel of the instant of time, the moment
of experience or of recollection. In the elegies, the
poetry does achieve the full exposure and exploration.
In some other poems, its meaning eludes, or resists. But
so long as the 'moment' is present, how moving the
poetry often is! Consider the stylish opening of *An
Ancient to Ancients*, so soon to vanish in the labour of
exposition. Or consider how *A Night of Questionings*
opens, with what assurance in the rhythms, and with
what concentration of the feeling by strong imagery.

> On the even of All-Souls' Day
> I heard the dead men say
> Who lie by the tottering tower,

To the dark and doubling wind
At the midnight's turning hour,
When other speech had thinned:
  'What of the world now?'
The wind whiffed back: 'Men still
Who are born, do good, do ill
Here, just as in your time:
Till their years the locust hath eaten,
Leaving them bare, downbeaten;
Somewhiles in springtide rime,
Somewhiles in summer glow,
Somewhiles in winter snow:—
  No more I know.'

The later statements of the poem cannot sustain this impressiveness; but here, responding to the temporary impact, are all the contributory elements of Hardy's poetic art: the fundamental grave-ironic seriousness, the vivid sense of time and place made suddenly resonant (the tottering tower, the dark and doubling wind, the midnight's turning hour), the apprehension of the seasonal rhythm, the personal idiosyncrasies jostling the biblical memories.

Occasionally the poetry is immersed altogether in the athletic sensation of the 'moment', as in the delicate *Snow in the Suburbs*, or *On Sturminster Foot-bridge*, whose language is at first disconcerting in its range and vigour.

Reticulations creep upon the slack stream's face
  When the wind skims irritably past,
The current clucks smartly into each hollow place
That years of flood have scrabbled in the pier's sodden base;
  The floating-lily leaves rot fast.

One becomes aware, in terms of words and things, of Hardy's steady refusal to discountenance any quality of life or experience as material for poetic art. He does not manage a diction in which the words can be at ease,

> . . . where every word is at home,
> Taking its place to support the others,
> The word neither diffident nor ostentatious,
> An easy commerce of the old and the new,
> The common word exact without vulgarity,
> The formal word precise but not pedantic,
> The complete consort dancing together.

That is poetic diction, and that dancing of the consort
Hardy rarely achieved. But with or without the dancing,
he draws upon every verbal resource, ever pursuing the
'closeness of phrase to his vision' that he himself celebrated in the poetry of Barnes. Seeking to eliminate
from his own language what that Dorsetshire poet and
philologist would have regarded as corruption of language, or abstraction of language from thing, he constructs
a speech of truculent sincerity.

Perhaps the most important of this group of poems
are those in which Hardy's special feeling towards
shadow and gloom, the falling of light, declares itself.
(The striking stage-settings of *The Dynasts* return constantly to the sensation of gradual darkness; there is a
superb passage on the flight after Jena, fog curtaining
all.) *Nobody Comes*, ostensibly dealing simply with the
passing of a car through the darkness, seems to achieve
a boding significance when

> . . . the fainting light
> Succumbs to the crawl of night. . . .

But *An August Midnight*, qualified success though it be,
is even more interesting because it illuminates Hardy's
private consciousness of just this element in his art.

> A shaded lamp and a waving blind,
> And the beat of a clock from a distant floor:
> On this scene enter—winged, horned, and spined—
> A longlegs, a moth, and a dumbledore;

> While 'mid my pages there idly stands
> A sleepy fly, that rubs its hands . . .

> Thus meet we five, in this still place,
> At this point of time, at this point in space . . .

A part of Hardy's unique quality resides in his response to these: the clock, the darkness, the point in time, the point in space; in his power to invest poetry with this presentness of the present moment. The falling of light is the main thread in his imagery, a simple and suggestive one; sometimes it is itself the 'moment' and usually it carries undertones of loneliness, of regret, of loss. So it is in that quiet-voiced, modest poem, *A Commonplace Day*:

> The day is turning ghost,
> And scuttles from the kalendar in fits and furtively,
>   To join the anonymous host
> Of those that throng oblivion; ceding his place, maybe,
>   To one of like degree.

> I part the fire-gnawed logs,
> Rake forth the embers, spoil the busy flames, and lay the ends
>   Upon the shining dogs;
> Further and further from the nooks the twilight's stride
>   extends,
>   And beamless black impends. . . .

The twilight awakens some anonymous regret; it coincides with the moment so directly recorded in *After a Journey*.

> Hereto I come to view a voiceless ghost;
>   Whither, O whither will its whim now draw me?
> Up the cliff, down, till I'm lonely, lost,
>   And the unseen waters' ejaculations awe me. . . .

We may be allowed to describe this 'moment' in Hardy's poetry, suddenly profound, its very identity noted, as a foreshadowing, or an after-falling, of that peculiar emotion of regret, and that insight into the desolation of utter loss that is Hardy's deepest theme, and out of which he has made a poetry, not massive, nor assured, yet original and his own; speaking with a quiet voice in the tradition of our poetry, but leaving a permanent accent upon its language.

V

THESE, then, may be said to constitute Hardy's poetic personality: the endowments of the trained balladist and folk singer; the habitual severe acknowledgement of all that honest experience reports; the impulse of nostalgia; and the poignant sensation of the present moment. It is not surprising that such a poet should find his gifts peculiarly apposite to the demands of elegy. Consider *The Self-Unseeing*:

> Here is the ancient floor,
> Footworn and hollowed and thin,
> Here was the former door
> Where the dead feet walked in.
>
> She sat here in her chair,
> Smiling into the fire;
> He who played stood there,
> Bowing it higher and higher.
>
> Childlike, I danced in a dream;
> Blessings emblazoned that day;
> Everything glowed with a gleam;
> Yet we were looking away!

It is songlike, yet substantial; its feeling accords with an equable rhythm of regretful acceptance—this is how things go for everyone: yet the inner movement is personal and subtle. *Overlooking the river Stour* is like this. *Friends Beyond* and *Exeunt Omnes* are even more communal and acquiescent, yet a distinct and personal movement works through each. Some of the elegies, early and later, are dramatic fantasies. They take in imagined loss a starting point for feeling again and meditating the transitoriness to which Hardy responds so strongly and directly. Some honour particular people: his mother, Leslie Stephen, George Meredith; others muse over the death of a pet dog or cat. And there are some elegies, and brief poems of regret, composed before 1912, that seem to start from his own relationship with his wife. They seem to apprehend that loss of her, perhaps subversively desired by one part of his nature yet foreseen by another part of him as inexpressibly poignant: they seem to be trying out what it should feel like, or preparing that mood of deep self-questioning that was to follow Emma's death. *The Division*, of 1893, is such a poem.

There are many fine poems among such elegies as these, and some less fine. But looking over Hardy's work as a whole it is possible to see all these (or nearly all) as in a certain sense experimental only. They do the hard work of practice that might keep a channel clear and ready for when life should make its irresistible claim upon him, and when elegy should be elegy in earnest, elegy rising out of a humanly demanding situation. From the death of Emma Hardy there came the small collection with which he commemorated their love and his loss, *Vestigia Veteris Flammae*, the elegies of 1912–13—to which should be added two or three more of the same years, scattered in later volumes: notably *The Dream is—Which?* and *When Oats were Reaped*. Here, as I think, is Hardy's supreme achievement in poetry; among these are his finest single poems.

It is as well to be clear about the place of Hardy's
private experience in our reading of these poems. We
recall the growing distress that attended the last years
of their marriage, Hardy's feeling of division between
them, his dismay, his powerlessness to alter things. We
may think of his bewilderment, and pain, at her vanity,
her waywardness, her frigidity; and how vexed he was
by her snobbery, her preference for that in the life of
the social élite of London which he found mannered and
null. Most of all we should remember the particular
dread and insecurity occasioned by the periods of insanity. Hardy leaves us in no doubt that the lonely year
at Max Gate that followed her death included feelings of
profound relief. But (the poems themselves tell us
openly) such feelings were subtly compounded with
painful feelings of responsibility.

> That day when oats were reaped, and wheat was ripe, and
> barley ripening,
> The road-dust hot, and the bleaching grasses dry,
> I walked along and said,
> While looking just ahead to where some silent people lie:
>
> 'I wounded one who's there, and now know well I wounded
> her;
> But, ah, she does not know that she wounded me!'
> And not an air stirred
> Nor a bill of any bird; and no response accorded she.

When, in his own phrase, the scales fell from his eyes, it
was less her part in the division he questioned, than his
own. And 'the verses came; it was quite natural. One
looked back through the years and saw some pictures; a
loss like that makes one's old brain vocal.' Even in the
way Hardy thinks aloud about it, apologises for the dis-

closed intimacies, and before we come to the verses themselves, we are made aware of an absence of self-concern, self-projection, even though these poems come from the most personal grief life inflicted on him. And not surprisingly, this is the very character of the poems. The loss matters as itself; it does not matter on his behalf, because it happened to him. Where the self is concerned, the loss occasions questioning, accusation even, regarding the part the living husband had played. There is no self-defence, no self-regard; grief, regret, memory, speak to him of the nature of things, of how life goes for everyone. There is not even the beginning of an appeal for condolence. From this comes the depth and strength we gradually perceive in these elegies. Loss has brought about a responsible, perplexed self-searching, and with that an unassuming recognition of oneself simply as a representative human being.

So it comes about that the particular distinction of the elegies is their *dramatic* vitality, something other than the lyric pressure usual in verse of this kind. The poems may lodge in personal memories and in recollections that came unbidden upon the consciousness, but the peculiar excellence lies in the disengagement of the self. There may be an 'I', named or speaking, for this loss has happened; but the grief does not turn inward upon 'I, Thomas Hardy' nor ask attention for him. Indeed, a number of the poems in *Veteris *Vestigia Flammae* stop short and break off at just the moment when the grief seems about to become self-regarding. The emotion, deep as it is, remains germane to the presented occasion, and the distress is given off as the flavour of that situation, a constituent of the memories there realized: not a cause of them nor an excuse for them. And the distress is complex, it includes the sense of failure to understand and respond to opportunity when opportunity offered.

Loss here is not merely loss of a person; it is a foregoing of means to repair error, an admission that the relationship cannot now be made worthier or finer than it was. These poems take the measure of all that, without striking attitudes, unaffectedly. It is a commonplace that to strike an attitude, play a part, present the self in the grief-stricken attitude taken up, is the insidious temptation when poetry treats of grief. Hardy's achievement—it may be called a moral achievement—is to have composed that kind of poetry as if unaware even of the temptation. He remains most naturally himself when most deeply distressed.

Take the first poem of the series, and one of the finest of all, *The Going*. The distress, the danger to poetic integrity, need no further emphasis once we have read to the end. But the marvellous inner poise holds firm. At first the memory seems veritably to loiter with the small particulars out of which the elegiac statement rises. There is no pretence to the strong containment of grief (one possible attitude), but if the memories are not refused, neither does any touch inflate them or invest them with a tragic aura. The sense of fact is extraordinary, and to have got this presence of the musing voice into poetry is itself an achievement. The poem scarcely needs to be read, it speaks. What, then, does the profounder work? Isn't it the inner rhythm that gradually disturbs and finally collapses the lilt and movement of folksong? For the last verse to act as it does, this more formal, gentle, communal movement needed time to tell; and even while it is telling, the sharp presence of detail and occurrence as they come back upon memory, brings the inner rhythm to life. It is a rhythm, once there, that wholly commits words and phrases to the structure of feeling they represent. It is a rhythm, too, which we can identify as a supremely natural use of the conversing or the self-communing voice.

> Why, then, latterly did we not speak,
> Did we not think of those days long dead,
> And ere your vanishing strive to seek
> That time's renewal? We might have said,
>   'In this bright spring weather
>   We'll visit together
> Those places that once we visited.'

> Well, well! All's past amend,
>   Unchangeable. It must go.
> I seem but a dead man held on end
> To sink down soon. . . O you could not know
>   That such swift fleeing
>   No soul foreseeing—
> Not even I—would undo me so!

Throughout the poem, as we look back on it from that final vantage point, simple words, odd words, little colloquial pushes, exist in a unique way for their use here. What may strike us as mere idiosyncrasy, or innocent clumsiness, reveals itself as bearing the tang of peculiarly distinct perception ('saw morning harden upon the wall') or as the delicate indication of a human predicament less simple than at first it seemed.

Mr. R. P. Blackmur's essay in *Language as Gesture* is perhaps the most helpful consideration of Hardy's poetry that has yet appeared. I wish to quote at this point his discussion of *The Walk* from *Veteris Vestigia Flammae*, and of a later elegy, both for the support it offers to the account of Hardy's distinction just suggested, and for the eloquence with which the case is put. Mr. Blackmur writes of the set of approaches given us in *Last Words to a Dumb Friend* as 'all direct, all personal,

amounting to the creation or release of objective
experience.' And he continues:

> Let us observe the stages of approach, not to explain the
> process but to expand our sense of participation in it. First
> there is the selectively detailed materialization of what it
> was that died: purrer of the spotless hue with the plumy
> tail, that would stand, arched, to meet the stroking hand.
> After the tenderness of immediate memory comes the first
> reaction: never to risk it again.

> > Better bid his memory fade,
> > Better blot each mark he made,
> > Selfishly escape distress
> > By contrived forgetfulness,
> > Than preserve his prints to make
> > Every morn and eve an ache.

Then come eight lines which envisage what must be done,
and the impossibility of doing it, to blot the memory out.
All this Hardy supplied, as it were, by a series of directly
felt observations; and these, in their turn, released one of
those deeply honest, creative visions of man in relation to
death which summoned the full imagination in Hardy as
nothing else could.

> > Strange it is this speechless thing, . . .
> > Should—by crossing at a breath
> > Into safe and shielded death,
> > By the merely taking hence
> > Of his insignificance—
> > Loom as largened to the sense,
> > Shape as part, above man's will,
> > Of the Imperturbable.

> > As a prisoner, flight debarred,
> > Exercising in a yard,

Still retain I, troubled, shaken,
Mean estate, by him forsaken;
And this home, which scarcely took
Impress from his little look,
By his faring to the Dim.
Grows all eloquent of him.

Housemate I can think you still
Bounding to the window-sill,
Over which I vaguely see
Your small mound beneath the tree,
Showing in the autumn shade
That you moulder where you played.

Andrew Marvell hardly did better; and the end rises like the whole of Yeats's *A Deep-sworn Vow*. You can say, if you like, that all Hardy had to do was to put it down, which explains nothing and begs the question of poetic process which we want to get at. What should be emphasized is, that in putting it down, Hardy used no violence of intellect or predilection; the violence is inside, working out, like the violence of life or light. The burden of specific feeling in the first part of the poem set enough energy up to translate the thought in the second half to the condition of feeling; and the product of the two is the poetic emotion which we feel most strongly as the rhythm, not the pattern-rhythm of the lines, but the invoked rhythm, beating mutually in thought, and feeling and syllable, of the whole poem.

Rhythm, in that sense, is the great enacting agent of actuality in poetry, and appears seldom, without regard to goodwill or application. . . . *Veteris Vestigia Flammae* give, as a unit, Hardy's most sustained invocation of that rhythm, so strong that all that was personal—the private drive, the private grief—is cut away, and the impersonal is left bare, an old monument, mutilated or weathered as you like to call it, of that face which the personal only hides. Here, for example, is one of the shorter, called *The Walk*.

You did not walk with me
Of late to the hill-top tree
   By the gated ways,
   As in earlier days;
   You were weak and lame,
   So you never came,
And I went alone, and I did not mind,
Not thinking of you as left behind.

I walked up there to-day
Just in the former way;
   Surveyed around
   The familiar ground
   By myself again:
   What difference, then?
Only that underlying sense
Of the look of a room on returning thence.

Like the others in the series, it is a poem almost without
style; it is style reduced to anonymity, reduced to riches;
in the context of the other twenty, precisely the riches of
rhythm.

This seems to me entirely just. And in the context of
such poetry it may be right to set a question mark
against one or two of the famous pieces often named
among Hardy's greatest: *Neutral Tones*, for instance, and
A Broken Appointment. Murry's essay in *Aspects of Literature*
first elevated *Neutral Tones*, and both are among the
very short list of poems by which Dr. F. R. Leavis in
New Bearings in English Poetry substantiates his claims for
Hardy's stature. It is my own experience that repeated
return to these displaces them. They seem not to be
unequivocally fine as the later elegies are, and for the
most significant of reasons. They have the grand manner.
The poems of 1912–13 really are 'almost without style'
but there is more than a touch of style about those two

poems; along with the pathos there goes the gesture of importance, behind the eloquence stand Shakespeare— and Swinburne. It is the assumption of the grand manner that the really distinguished Hardy elegies forgo.

The conspicuous triumphs to be named with *The Going* are, surely, *The Voice*, *After a Journey*, and *At Castle Boterel*. The first two stand in close relation. In *The Voice* the action of the poem as a breakdown of the rhythm of folksong into bare, grieved utterance of the musing voice is more dramatic, indeed more over- whelmingly poignant than it is in *The Going*. But the suddenness is of the surface. Beneath, we feel the troubling currents long before the change. Dr. Leavis has pointed to the modification of an easy song rhythm by something more subtle and personal:

> Can it be you that I hear? Let me view you, then,
> Standing as when I drew near to the town
> Where you would wait for me: yes, as I knew you then
> Even to the original air-blue gown!

Here, too, particularities of memory summon out the personal rhythm. In the third verse an unsure, faltering movement responds to the listless breeze, and at the same time forebodes the final bewildered tremour. What we have in that last verse is an enactment of the present moment in all its isolated and unalterable pre- sentness. The sensation of loss, the faltering of spirit and body alike, joins with the very sound of the wind that had projected a voice upon the ear. Its sound is bewilderingly confused with the voice out of the past that had seemed even more present than this desolation until a moment ago. We may feel the faltering, with the recognition of how things really are, act out its for- lorn movement through the consciousness.

Or is it only the breeze, in its listlessness
Travelling across the wet mead to me here,
You being ever dissolved to existlessness,
Heard no more again far or near?

Thus I; faltering forward,
Leaves around me falling,
Wind oozing thin through the thorn from norward
And the woman calling.

After a Journey is the most subtle of the four, particularly in the delicacy with which it focuses and aligns the elusive values the past has to offer the present. The bewildering potency of memory is here, but unobtrusively controlled by a steadfast acknowledgement of time present; not something rising through the rhythm to disturb its outward pattern finally as in the first two poems, but gently there always. Equally there is acknowledgement of the 'ghostly' 'flitting' quality of past joy and past relationship. It is precisely this 'flitting' quality with which memory beguiles and tantalizes: and for this same quality of elusive bodilessness, such possession as one may momentarily secure feels doubly precious. Although the personal *claim* upon us is nowhere a pressure, yet in no other poem (I find) do we stand so near to Hardy himself, a diffident, bereaved man moving in a darkness both physical and spiritual; dismayed about his part in an irreparable relationship; and at the beck and call of shifting perspectives of reminiscence, recollection, musing; from the second and third lines onward, disorientated; and from the end of the first verse, as it were dizzied. Yet this is not the right word. For the dead person and the encounters come upon the consciousness with peculiar definition. The 'ghost' is

> Facing round about me everywhere
> With your nut-coloured hair
> And gray eyes, and rose-flush coming and going. . .

—and so is much more than 'ghost'. The figure in the
present moment, 'lonely, lost,' who tracks the phantom
through the unsteady movements of the lines, is hardly
less distinct. And the phantom is lively, pre-occupying:
and yet is the woman whose very absence as a living
person constitutes the desolate present time. Thus the
poem constructs a balance that trembles between two
realities. There are the 'olden haunts' and 'the unseen
waterfall' and the glowing vitality of the once-living
woman: all that memory preserves. And there are the
darkness and emptiness of the lonely present, and of the
unfulfilled possibilities of so long a relationship.

> Yes: I have re-entered your olden haunts at last;
>   Through the years, through the dead scenes I have tracked
>   you;
> What have you now found to say of our past—
>   Scanned across the dark space wherein I have lacked you?
> Summer gave us sweets, but autumn wrought division?
>   Things were not lastly as firstly well
>   With us twain, you tell?
> But all's closed now, despite Time's derision.
>
> I see what you are doing: you are leading me on
>   To the spots we knew when we haunted here together,
> The waterfall, above which the mist-bow shone
>   At the then fair hour in the then fair weather,
> And the cave just under, with a voice still so hollow
>   That it seems to call out to me from forty years ago,
>   When you were all aglow,
> And not the thin ghost that I now fraily follow!

Then the present moment defines itself in an act of
profound realization, and in another way than the way

N

of *The Going* and *The Voice*. Memory has not beguiled;
it is acknowledged with gratitude, for it provides what
small resource there is· for perpetuating life's most
prized experience into the present. There has been no
deception. From the first line of the poem wide-open
eyes, eyes that have got used to the dark, have been
'viewing,' 'scanning'. This watchfulness of the tracker,
bewildered but alert in the haunted places, can distinguish with integrity the fact from the fiction and the
fact in the fiction, and can value both. So in this last
verse the present is received with equanimity. There is
no alteration of pattern, no rising of a different rhythm,
for here there is no need. The 'preening' of bird and
the 'flopping' of seal make their own effect upon the
wilful phantom. But its vanishing means both a coming
and a going of light. The stars close their shutters, and
the dawn whitens hazily—the last word preserving still
that note of bewilderment, of dizziness amid shifting
perspectives, given out at the beginning. The dawn
'whitens' with the numb, colourless aspect of the
grieved self that must concede the illusoriness of the
visitation, face out time's derision, and meet the dawn
of days still to be lived through alone.

> Ignorant of what there is flitting here to see,
>   The waked birds preen and the seals flop lazily;
> Soon you will have, Dear, to vanish from me,
>   For the stars close their shutters and the dawn whitens
>   hazily.
> Trust me, I mind not, though Life lours,
>   The bringing me here; nay, bring me here again!
>   I am just the same as when
> Our days were a joy, and our paths through flowers.

The pattern in *At Castle Boterel* is only a little different.
First the trivial, apparently accidental particulars of

recollection, seen 'distinctly yet'; then the memory distends in the mind. The short statements begin to move across the metrical pattern, itself contracting and expanding. Out of the distension of memory the assessment comes, honourable and dignified. And finally the poem returns to the particular, to a person in the present moment. These last two verses may well end this account, for they are perfectly in character. The most natural use of the words and movement of talk, unaffected and with no raising of the voice, blends tenderly into the language of community: those folksong phrases into which the self vanishes, so that a merely representative man speaks for all men. Who else in English poetry, we might ask, could have given the statement 'I look back at it amid the rain' quite the potency it has here?

> And to me, though Time's unflinching rigour,
>   In mindless rote, has ruled from sight
> The substance now, one phantom figure
>   Remains on the slope, as when that night
>   Saw us alight.
>
> I look and see it there, shrinking, shrinking,
>   I look back at it amid the rain
> For the very last time; for my sand is sinking,
>   And I shall traverse old love's domain
>   Never again.

SELECT BIBLIOGRAPHY
(Place of publication London, unless stated otherwise)

BIBLIOGRAPHY

THOMAS HARDY. A Bibliographical Study. By Richard L. Purdy (1954).

COLLECTED EDITIONS

WORKS IN PROSE AND VERSE (Pocket Edition). 25 vols. (1906–19).

WORKS IN PROSE AND VERSE (Mellstock Edition). 37 vols. (1919–20).

THE NOVELS (Library Edition) now in progress. This edition will eventually comprise all Hardy's works.

COLLECTED SHORT STORIES (1928).

COLLECTED POEMS (1952). This edition, in one volume, includes all of Hardy's poetry, but not *The Dynasts* or *The Queen of Cornwall*.

SEPARATE WORKS
I. *Novels*

THE POOR MAN AND THE LADY (1868). Never published; and, in its original form, beyond recovery.

DESPERATE REMEDIES (1871).

UNDER THE GREENWOOD TREE—A rural Painting of the Dutch School (1872).

A PAIR OF BLUE EYES (1873).

FAR FROM THE MADDING CROWD (1874).

THE HAND OF ETHELBERTA—a Comedy in Chapters (1876).

THE RETURN OF THE NATIVE (1878).

THE TRUMPET-MAJOR—A Tale (1880).

A LAODICEAN—or, The Castle of the De Stancys. A Story of To-day (1881).

TWO ON A TOWER—A Romance (1882).

THE MAYOR OF CASTERBRIDGE: The Life and Death of a Man of Character (1886).

THE WOODLANDERS (1887).

TESS OF THE D'URBERVILLES: A Pure Woman faithfully Presented (1891).

JUDE THE OBSCURE (1896).

THE WELL-BELOVED—A Sketch of a Temperament (1897).

II. *Collections of Stories*

WESSEX TALES: Strange, Lively, and Commonplace (1888).

A GROUP OF NOBLE DAMES (1891).

LIFE'S LITTLE IRONIES. A Set of Tales with some Colloquial Sketches entitled 'A Few Crusted Characters' (1894).

A CHANGED MAN, THE WAITING SUPPER, AND OTHER TALES (1913).

The collections of stories are somewhat arbitrarily made, and bear no relation to the order of composition. A chronological index of all the stories follows this bibliography.

III. *Collections of Poems, and Dramatic Works*

WESSEX POEMS and other Verses (1898).

POEMS OF THE PAST AND PRESENT (1901).

THE DYNASTS. A Drama of the Napoleonic Wars. Three Parts (1903-4, 1906, 1908).

TIME'S LAUGHING STOCKS AND OTHER VERSES (1909).

SATIRES OF CIRCUMSTANCE. Lyrics and Reveries (1914).

MOMENTS OF VISION and Miscellaneous Verses (1917).

LATE LYRICS AND EARLIER. With many other Verses (1922).

THE FAMOUS TRAGEDY OF THE QUEEN OF CORNWALL AT TINTAGEL IN LYONNESS (1923).

HUMAN SHOWS, FAR PHANTASIES. SONGS AND TRIFLES (1925).

WINTER WORDS, in Various Moods and Metres (1928).

The Collections of Poems have little chronological significance. The *Poems of 1912–13, Veteris Vestigia Flammae*, are to be found in SATIRES OF CIRCUMSTANCE. A list of the poems referred to in this book, giving the date of composition where that is known, follows this bibliography.

IV. *Selected Essays and Articles*

LIFE AND ART. New York (1925). A collection of essays, notes, and letters not previously printed in book form. Edited with an introduction by E. Brennecke.

THE DORSETSHIRE LABOURER (1883). *Longmans Magazine.*

THE DORSET FARM LABOURER, PAST AND PRESENT (1884). Dorchester.

THE REV. WILLIAM BARNES (1886) *The Athenaeum.*

THE PROFITABLE READING OF FICTION (1888). *The Forum.* New York.

CANDOUR IN ENGLISH FICTION (1890). *The New Review.*

THE SCIENCE OF FICTION (1981). *The New Review.*

PREFACE TO SELECT POEMS OF WILLIAM BARNES (1908).

BIOGRAPHICAL STUDIES

THE EARLY LIFE OF THOMAS HARDY, 1840–91, by F. E. Hardy (1928).

THE LATER YEARS OF THOMAS HARDY, 1892–1928, by F. E. Hardy (1930).
These two volumes comprise the standard biography of Hardy. They include the only selections from his letters and notebooks that have so far been published.

HARDY OF WESSEX. His Life and Literary Career, by C. J. Weber. New York (1940). In spite of the fresh material it uses, this biography is too wayward to be read without great caution.

THOMAS HARDY, by Edmund Blunden. *English Men of Letters Series.* (1941). Although necessarily brief, this deeply sympathetic book contains the best biography available.

THOMAS HARDY, by Evelyn Hardy (1954). A full modern biography, together with critical observations upon Hardy's works.

CRITICAL STUDIES

THE ART OF THOMAS HARDY, by Lionel Johnson (1894).
A new edition of this study, still the most revealing account
of the novels, appeared in 1923, with supplementary
material.

THE HARDY COUNTRY, by C. G. Harper (1904).

THOMAS HARDY: A CRITICAL STUDY, by Lascelles Abercrombie
(1912).

A STUDY OF THOMAS HARDY, by D. H. Lawrence (1914)
posthumously published in *Phoenix*.

THOMAS HARDY: A STUDY OF THE WESSEX NOVELS, by H. C.
Duffin (1916). A new edition, with supplementary material,
appeared in 1937.

THE POETRY OF THOMAS HARDY, by J. M. Murry (1919).
Articles first printed in the *Athenaeum*, and later published in
Aspects of Literature.

SCIENCE AND POETRY, by I. A. Richards (1926). Contains
a valuable section on Hardy's poetry.

THOMAS HARDY. A critical study, by A. S. MacDowell (1931).

NEW BEARINGS IN ENGLISH POETRY, by F. R. Leavis (1932).
Contains a valuable section on Hardy's poetry.

HARDY THE NOVELIST, by F. Chapman (1934). An important
article published in *Scrutiny*.

THOMAS HARDY. A Study of his Writings and their Background,
by W. R. Rutland.

HARDY THE NOVELIST, by Lord David Cecil (1943).

HARDY'S MEPHISTOPHELIAN VISITANTS, by J. O. Bailey (1946).
An article published in the P.M.L.A.

THE POETRY OF THOMAS HARDY, by J. G. Southworth (1947).

ON A DARKLING PLAIN. The Art and Thought of Thomas
Hardy, by H. C. Webster (1947).
Together with Dr. Rutland's book mentioned above, this
contains the most valuable material on the intellectual
background to Hardy's life and work.

THE INTEGRITY OF HARDY, by J. I. M. Stewart (1948). An
important article published in *English Studies*.

THOMAS HARDY: THE NOVELS AND STORIES, by A. J. Guerard
(1949).

Although, in the view of the present writer, erratic in its assessments, this is by far the most perceptive and stimulating recent study of Hardy's fiction.

THE NOVELS OF THOMAS HARDY, in *Essays on Literature and Society*, by Edwin Muir (1949).

DORSET HARDY, by L. A. G. Strong (1951). An article published in *Essays in Criticism*.

REALITY AND SINCERITY, by F. R. Leavis (1952). A further important study of Hardy's poetry, in *Scrutiny*.

THE VICTORIAN SAGE, by J. Holloway (1953). Contains an excellent assessment of Hardy as thinker and moralist.

THE LYRICAL POETRY OF THOMAS HARDY (The Warton Lecture, 1953), by C. Day Lewis.

LANGUAGE AS GESTURE, by R. P. Blackmur (1954). Contains an important chapter on Hardy's poetry.

Note: Some reference ought to be made to the *Hardy Centennial Issue* of the *Southern Review*, Summer 1940. Many of the essays there collected are unusually penetrating and forthright, the work of distinguished American critics.

BACKGROUND STUDIES

THE GAMEKEEPER AT HOME (1878), HODGE AND HIS MASTERS, and ROUND ABOUT A GREAT ESTATE (1880), by Richard Jefferies.

RURAL ENGLAND, by Sir H. Rider Haggard (1902).

CHANGE IN THE VILLAGE, and THE WHEELWRIGHT'S SHOP, by George Bourne (1912 and 1923).

FICTION AND THE READING PUBLIC, by Q. D. Leavis (1939).

VILLAGE LIFE AND LABOUR, by C. G. Hutchinson and F. Chapman (1939). This excellent documentary contains a short bibliography of the subject.

THE ENGLISH VILLAGE, by V. Bonham-Carter (1952).

INDEX

Abercrombie, Lascelles, 102, 108

Addison, Joseph, 103

Amaryllis at the Fair, 142

American Civil War, 32

Apologia Pro Vita Sua (Newman), 5

Arch, Joseph, 33, 41

Attic Tragedy, 4, 20, 27

Art of Thomas Hardy, The (Lionel Johnson), 18

Balliol Players, 27

Barnes, William, 3, 154, 158, 168

Bergson, Henri, 26

Blackmur, R. P., 175

Blomfield, Arthur, 4, 6

Blunden, Edmund, 2, 10, 26, 104, 134

Bockhampton, 1, 5, 8, 12, 16

Boscastle, 7

Browning, Robert, 145, 154–5

Cakes and Ale, 101

Cambridge, 26

Chapman and Hall, 6

Collins, Wilkie, 6

Conrad, Joseph, 142

Cornhill, The, 12, 14

Corn Laws, 35, 70

Cornwall, 17

Crabbe, George, 20, 116

Crimean War, 32

Darwin, Charles, 21

Defoe, Daniel, 120

Dewey Morn, The, 142

Dickens, Charles, 139

Disraeli, Benjamin, 32–3

Dorchester (including references to 'Casterbridge'), 2, 5, 7, 15, 27–8, 64, 66–8, 88, 102

Dorchester Players, 27

Driffield, Edward (*Cakes and Ale*), 101

Dugdale, Florence (afterwards Mrs. F. E. Hardy), 11, 15, 25, 88, 91, 99

Eliot, George, 89, 110

Eliot, T. S., 73

Fielding, Henry, 120

Franco-Prussian War, 32, 34

Free Trade, 31–2, 36

German Metaphysics, 17, 22, 72, 111

Gifford, Emma Lavinia (afterwards Mrs. E. L. Hardy), 7, 9, 14, 16, 18–19, 24–5, 171 ff.

Gosse, Edmund, 13, 17

Granville-Barker, Harley, G., 26

Great Exhibition, 117–18

Guerard, Albert J., 10

Haggard, Sir H. Rider, 31, 36, 38–9

Hardy, Thomas (father), 1, 18

Hardy, Mrs. Jemima (mother) 2, 23, 171

Hardy, Thomas,
 I. Life:
  Early experiences, 2; training as an architect, 3–4; life in London, 4–5; literary aspirations, 5; writes *The Poor Man and the Lady*, 6; publishes *Desperate Remedies* at own expense, 7; sells *Under the Greenwood Tree* to Tinsley, 9; tragedy of Horace Moule, 11; influence of Leslie Stephen, 11; writes *Far from the Madding Crowd*, and accepts other commissions, 12; marriage, and happiness at Sturminster Newton, 12–13; *Return of the Native* appears, 14; improving position, 15; builds and moves to Max Gate, 15; novels written in the country, 16; unhappiness of married life, 17; *Tess* appears, 17; impact of *Jude*, 19; first volume of poetry, and preparation of *The Dynasts*, 20; intellectual and spiritual development, 20–2; Order of Merit, 24; death of first wife,

25; re-marriage, 26; honoured
in old age, 25–7; later volumes
of poetry, 27–8; death, 28
II. Works: (a) Novels:
Novels of Character and Environ-
   ment, 32, 36, 45–100, 111,
   141–3, 146
The Poor Man and the Lady, 6–7,
   120
Desperate Remedies, 7
Under the Greenwood Tree (at
   first called The Mellstock Quire),
   8–9, 12, 30, 45–8, 55
Far from the Madding Crowd, 9,
   12, 16, 30, 48–55, 56, 71,
   109, 140
A Pair of Blue Eyes, 10, 134, 140
The Hand of Ethelberta, 12
The Return of the Native, 13–14,
   16, 30, 55–63, 72, 105, 109,
   111, 128
The Trumpet-Major, 14, 30, 55,
   112–15
A Laodicean, 14
Two on a Tower, 15
The Mayor of Casterbridge, 15–16,
   27, 30, 35, 63–70, 101, 113,
   131, 140, 146
The Woodlanders, 16, 30, 41,
   55, 60, 70–89, 98, 104, 127
Tess, 17, 30, 35–6, 40–1, 55,
   85, 89–98, 111, 137
Jude, 18, 30, 36, 89, 90, 98–100,
   120
The Well-Beloved, 19
   (b) Short Stories:
Collected Short Stories, 115–19
Wessex Tales, 110
Life's Little Ironies, 116
The Three Strangers, 110, 115
The Distracted Preacher, 115
The Romantic Adventures of a
   Milkmaid, 115, 117
A Few Crusted Characters, 115
Fellow Townsmen, 116
Interlopers at the Knap, 116
The Waiting Supper, 116–17
The Fiddler of the Reels, 117–18
Our Exploits at West Poley, 118
The Son's Veto, 118
   (c) Poems and Drama:

Collected Poems, 145–85, 164, 166
Wessex Poems, 22
Moments of Vision, 27
Winter Words, 28
During Wind and Rain, 147–52
Weathers, 154
Her Death and After, 155
Friends Beyond, 155
Channel Firing, 156–7
The Turnip Hoer, 157
The Dead Quire, 157–8
The Oxen, 158, 164
The Sleep-Walker, 160
The Darkling Thrush, 160–1
Afterwards, 162–3
The Impercipient, 163
Wessex Heights, 164
In a Wood, 165
To His Father's Violin, 165
In a Waiting Room, 166
A Night of Questionings, 166–7
On Sturminster Foot-bridge, 167
Nobody Comes, 168
An August Midnight, 168–9
A Commonplace Day, 169
After a Journey, 169
The Self-Unseeing, 170
Vestigia Veteris Flaminae, 171 ff.
When Oats were Reaped, 171–3
The Going, 174–5
Last Words to a Dumb Friend,
   175–7
The Walk, 177–8
The Voice, 179–80
At Castle Boterel, 182–3
The Dynasts, 20–3, 26, 161–2,
   168
The Queen of Cornwall, 27
   (d) Prose:
The Dorsetshire Labourer, 39–42,
   99, 137, 140
III. Analysis of Achievement:
As prose writer, 29, 101–6;
pattern of novels, 30; treat-
ment of agricultural tragedy,
37–8; nostalgia, 42, 98–9; treat-
ment of country voices, 107–9;
balladry and irony in his novels,
109–12; relation of novelist to
readers, 119; compared with
Wordsworth as tragic artist,

121–33; presentation of rural steadfastness and stoicism, 133–41; use of storm symbols, 52–4, 56, 75, 139–41; treatment of restoration through the agricultural environment, 84, 93, 94, 136–40, 142–3; summary of achievement as novelist, 141–3; general characteristics of poetry, 145–7; elements of folk verse, 153–9; readings of life in his poetry, 159–66; sense of the isolated moment in his poetry, 166–70; elegiac poetry, 170–83

IV. Chief Characters in the Novels:
Bridehead, Sue, 99
Charmond, Mrs., 74, 80, 85–6, 89
Clare, Angel, 92, 96, 137
Day, Fancy, 45–8
d'Urberville, Alec, 85, 91–2, 96, 98
Durbeyfield, Tess, 44, 54–5, 91–8, 137–8
Everdene, Bathsheba, 48–9, 51–2, 55, 71–2, 84, 86, 103, 109, 112, 135–7, 140
Farfrae, Donald, 43, 64–5, 68, 133
Fawley, Jude, 11, 98–100
Fitzpiers, Edred, 72–4, 79, 104, 126–7

Henchard, Michael, 42–4, 63–5, 67–8, 73, 131–3, 135, 140
Knight, Henry, 134, 140
Melbury, Grace, 16, 71–3, 76–7, 79–80, 82, 84, 86–7, 89, 104, 124–5
Melbury, Mr., 79–81, 83, 88–9
Newson, Elizabeth Jane, 132–3, 135
Oak, Gabriel, 42, 44, 48, 51–5, 63, 71, 75, 103, 112, 123, 129, 134–5, 140, 143
South, John, 85, 91–2, 112
South, Marty, 42, 71, 73–8, 80–5, 88, 112, 122, 124–7
Troy, Frank, 51–3, 114
Venn, Diggory, 56–8, 63, 72–3
Vye, Eustacia, 59, 61–2, 112

Winterborne, Giles, 44, 71–2, 76, 78–88, 104, 112, 122, 124–7, 140
Yeobright, Clym, 59–61, 73, 75, 84, 122
Yeobright, Mrs., 59, 61–2, 109

V. Places and Events referred to:
Bath, 51, 135
Casterbridge (see under Dorchester)
Egdon, 44, 55–6, 58, 60–3, 71, 75, 105, 128
Flintcomb Ash, 54–5, 90, 93–5, 138, 140
Hintock, 77, 85, 88
Hiring Fairs, 40–1
Lady Day Migrations, 40–1, 94, 97, 138–9
Marlott, 91, 93, 94
Mixen Lane, 67, 69
Rally, The (*Tess*), 93, 137
Sleepwalking Scene (*Tess*), 92, 94
Stonehenge, 90, 92, 111
Talbothays, 91, 95
Weatherbury, 51, 63, 71

Havelock Ellis, 15
Hicks, John, 3, 5–7, 88
Huxley, T. H., 5, 20, 21
Iliad, The, 4
In Memoriam (Tennyson), 170
Interloper, The, 25
Italy, 17

James, Henry, 44, 89
Job, The Book of, 127
Johnson, Lionel, 18, 30
Jefferies, Richard, 41, 142–3

Lawrence, D. H., 64, 99, 128, 134, 141–2
Leavis, F. R., 164, 178
Leavis, Q. D., 141

Macmillan, Alexander, 6, 8, 9, 17, 23
Macmillans' Magazine, 16, 17
Marcus Aurelius, 135
Maugham, Somerset, 101, 103, 106, 120
Max Gate, 15, 24–5, 27–8

Meredith, George, 6, 171
Michael (Wordsworth), 123, 129, 130-1
Mill, J. S., 5, 20-1
Moore, G. E., 26
Morgan, Charles, 27
Moule, C. W., 11
Moule, Horace, 3, 8, 11, 13, 20
Murray, John, 17
Murry, John Middleton, 152, 178

Napoleon, 14
National Agricultural Labourers' Union, 33, 35

Pound, Ezra, 20, 145-6
Powys, Llewellyn, 26
Pritchett, V. S., 39

R.I.B.A., 5, 27
Richards, I. A., 155, 159

Sassoon, Siegfried, 27
Saturday Review, 5
Scott, Sir Walter, 103, 120

Scrutiny, 130 n.
Shakespeare, William, 49, 154, 179
Smith, James, 130 n.
Society of Dorset Men in London, The, 23
Sophocles, 20
Spectator, The, 8, 12
Spencer, Herbert, 21
Stephen, Leslie, 11-14, 18-19, 21-2
Stinsford, 1, 27-8
Sturminster Newton, 13, 16
Swinburne, A. C., 154, 179

Times, The, 103, 120
Tinsley Bros., 7-9
Tinsley's Magazine, 9
Trevelyan, G. M., 39, 50

Waterloo, 161
Westminster Review, 15
Wordsworth, William, 121-4, 127, 129-30, 132

Yeats, W. B., 177